HOW DOES A PRO PLAY?

By *feel.* And so can you.

Once you learn to play by *feel,* you will make golf shots you never dreamed you could make. Long drives. Fine approaches. Wedge shots close to the flag.

You will merely visualize the type of shot you wish to play, summon the proper *feel* for that shot—and then simply swing the club.

Your subsconscious will provide you with the swing you need to execute the shot you have planned.

Bob Toski will show you how to get started toward the goal of every golfer—the "free" swing of the touring pro.

BOB TOSKI
with Dick Aultman
and the editors of Golf Digest

THE TOUCH SYSTEM FOR BETTER GOLF

Illustrations by Stan Drake

BANTAM BOOKS
TORONTO · NEW YORK · LONDON

THE TOUCH SYSTEM FOR BETTER GOLF

*A Bantam Book / published by arrangement with
Golf Digest, Inc.*

PRINTING HISTORY
Golf Digest edition published August 1971
2nd printing . . . April 1972   3rd printing . . . November 1972
4th printing . . . September 1973
Bantam edition published June 1974

CONTENTS

About Bob Toski

ONE
What this book is all about 4

TWO
Put your game into perspective 18

THREE
First steps toward better feel 34

FOUR
Building feel off the green 48

FIVE
How your swing should look 61

SIX
How your swing should feel 83

SEVEN
Make it work on the course 110

ABOUT DICK AULTMAN

Dick Aultman, 40, has been playing golf since the age of four and carries a 3 handicap. A former editor of *Golf Digest,* he has worked with most of the game's leading players and teachers on various instructional features. He has authored the bestselling book, *The Square-to-Square Golf Swing: Model Method for the Modern Player.*

ABOUT THE ILLUSTRATOR

Stan Drake, 51, illustrates the instructional Reminders that appear monthly in *Golf Digest.* He also creates the popular "Juliet Jones" cartoon strip, which appears daily in over 500 newspapers, and won the National Cartoonist Society's Outstanding Story Strip award in 1969 and 1970. Drake, a 7 handicap golfer, lives in Spain.

ABOUT BOB TOSKI

The World Championship of Golf was an extravaganza produced annually during the late 1940s and early 1950s by the late George S. May at Tam O'Shanter Country Club outside Chicago. First prize was $50,000, plus a guarantee for at least 50 exhibitions at $1,000 each, a total of $100,000 at a time when top money in most professional tournaments varied between $2,000 and $2,500.

That kind of money can shatter the nervous system of any golfer, even today, and Bob Toski, one of 13 children raised by Polish immigrant Walenty Algustoski, had every right to crack. Toski had started working for money when he was five, as shop boy to Al Porter at Northampton (Mass.) Country Club. By August 12, 1954, at 26, he had already gone broke twice on the pro tour. As he teed it up to start the fourth and final round of Mr. May's tournament, trailing the leader by just one shot, that $50,000 loomed very large indeed.

Millions of golfers watching on television that day saw Bob "win the world." And that's how many of them still remember him — as a player who won a big one. Actually, he had also captured five other tour events during the preceding 12 months. Following the exhibition tour, Bob gradually dropped out of steady competition to be with his family. Later he returned to national prominence in his current role as "expert analyst" on golf telecasts.

Those most closely affiliated with the world of golf, however, think of Bob Toski primarily in a role apart from those of player and television pundit. Those who play, teach, write about, or otherwise earn their living from golf, consider Toski one of the game's outstanding instructors. He is also regarded in this light by the thousands of "average

1

golfers" and the hundreds of top amateurs and professionals who have sought and received his help with their games

Toski is a "teaching professional" in the purest sense of the word. At Palmetto Dunes Resort and Golf Club, Hilton Head Island, S.C., Bob does not "run" the pro shops. He doesn't sell balls and shoes and culottes. Nor does he handle the books, store clubs, rent golf cars, or run club events.

What he does do, literally from dawn to dusk, six days a week, is teach golf — at $30 per hour, or proportionately more or less for longer or shorter lessons. Bob is devoted to his wife, Lynn, and their five children, and he also likes to putter around in the garden, and to watch other athletes perform in other sports. But what he thinks about most, even when he isn't teaching, is golf.

As editor of GOLF DIGEST magazine, I've had

many opportunities to experience the depth of Bob's understanding of the game. He has been a member of the magazine's Professional Panel since 1965, and, as such, has contributed dozens of instructional essays, usually written in longhand on lined note paper. I personally edited many of these contributions, but I really never appreciated fully Bob's talents for teaching the game until I began working with him on this book. Then his wonderful ability to communicate orally an exceptionally simple, yet novel, approach to teaching became more and more obvious.

Bob's basic teaching method is unusual in that he stresses how your swing should *feel,* rather than how it should *look.* He believes that once a player learns the overall feel of an effective swing, he or she will be more likely to duplicate that swing time after time than will the golfer who has been trained to arrive at certain positions, or to make certain "key moves," during the swing.

Bob's teaching approach will not confuse players who have had a more orthodox golfing education. The things that he stresses, such as visualizing shots beforehand, rhythm and proper timing, are vital to any type of swing, "one-piece," "Square-to-Square," or whatever.

My main functions were merely to take the most pertinent of Toski's observations, from the dozens of hours of taped interviews, and see that they followed one another in a logical order. By presenting Bob's words almost entirely as he actually spoke them, I hope to have communicated his insights and his enthusiasms so that you, the reader, will be "driven" toward the practice tee, just as I was so many times during the course of the project.

Dick Aultman
Norwalk, Conn.
May 1, 1974

CHAPTER ONE
WHAT THIS BOOK IS ABOUT

The first thing I'm going to do to make you a better golfer is ask that before you read any farther find yourself a pen or pencil and a piece of paper. Seriously! Go ahead. I'll wait.

Now, if you've done that, I'd like you to write your name three or four times *as fast and as legibly as you can.* I will do the same.

Let's compare signatures. I've reproduced mine here in the actual size that I wrote it. Are your handwriting strokes as light and as consistent as mine? Are your letters as tall and as deep and as wide? Or are your lines heavier, or your letters smaller? Does your handwriting seem as "free" as mine, or does it appear more "controlled."

And who do you think wrote the fastest, you or me? I'd better warn you that I've raced against dozens of "signature signers," and only a handful have written faster than I did. And none of them wrote as legibly.

What does all of this mean? Why did I ask you to write your name? I did so because I believe — I *know* — that there is a definite link between the way a person writes his name and the way he, or she, plays golf. I can watch a person sign his name, and then, almost invariably, describe correctly how he swings a golf club. The person who writes fast and smooth with big loops like I do usually makes a full, free, rhythmical swing, with his hands moving quite high on the backswing. The person who writes with a heavy-handed, jerky stroke and small letters usually has a relatively short, fast, jerky backswing.

Hold your pen or pencil as tight as you can and try to write your name. I'll bet that your writing suddenly becomes slower, and less legible than normal. Why? Because you overcontrol the pen. Then same thing happens when you over-control a golf club. Hold the clubhead too tight and you'll lose clubhead speed and rhythm. You won't hit the ball as far, or as straight.

Why can I drive a golf ball 250 or 260 yards and keep it in play almost every time? Certainly not because of my size or strength; I weigh barely 135 pounds when my wallet is full. That's why Sam Snead calls me "Mouse." I hit the ball far and straight simply because I have developed a high degree of *feel* for the rhythm and motion and timing of a proper swing. It's the same sensitivity for

The look of 'feel'
The uninhibited smooth-flowing motion of the expert's golf stroke usually reflects itself in his handwriting. Is your signature similarly free of heavy-handed jerkiness?

Playing by feel— the 'Touch System'

(Illustration 1) Once you learn to play by feel, you will successfully execute shot after shot with amazing consistency, because you will be relatively free from the conscious mental direction ("keep your head down") and negative thinking ("watch out for those trees on the left") that inhibits most swings. Upon mastering the "Touch System," you will plan and make shots as shown in the illustrations.

First, you will see and feel various aspects of the upcoming shot—how the ball looks sitting in the grass; how the wind feels on your face; how the terrain looks between the ball and the target; how the turf feels under your feet. You will feed this information to your "computer," your brain. With training, this feeding process will become almost automatic.

6

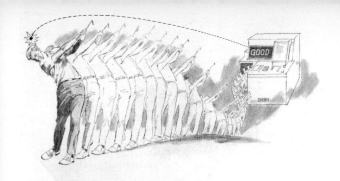

Next, you will "push the button," requesting your computer to feed you a visual image of the shot you'll need to make.

Next, you will summon forth the "feel" of making the shot you have visualized. Your computer can supply this feel because it has been programmed with the sight and feel of similar shots being successfully executed in the past. Part of the "Touch System" involves learning how to develop these "success patterns" and feed them to your subconscious.

Finally, with the feel for the proper swing dominating your mind and body, you will merely swing the club through the ball. Your subconscious will automatically make any adjustments in your swing that are necessary to produce the desired shot.

7

rhythm and motion that lets me write so fast and so legibly.

I know that with your cooperation I can teach you a similar feel for the proper golf swing. Once you develop this feel, you will make golf shots you never dreamed you could achieve, and with less effort than you now use.

I believe there are a FEW "mechanics" of golf — note the stress on "few" — that anyone who hopes to play well must first master. If you haven't already done so, you must learn, for instance, how to hold and aim the club, and how to align yourself to the ball and the target. I will explain these mechanics to give you the basis you need for your swing. You can't master high school algebra if you never learned first grade math.

But the main thrust of this book will be to teach you to play by *feel* — the Toski "Touch System." Mechanics will take you only so far. I strongly suspect that most people who read this book will have failed to reach their true potential as golfers because they have not gone beyond learning the mechanics of the swing. Most players get so wrapped up in mechanics — the so-called fundamental moves and key positions — that they never apply them with the freedom of movement and sensitivity of clubhead motion that allows a Chi Chi Rodriguez — or a Bob Toski — to hit drives 50 or 100 yards past men twice his size.

What we'll really be getting down to in this book is making you aware of your God-given abilities *to see* — yes, what you see has a tremendous influence on how you swing — and *to feel*. I'll tell you in many, many different ways how a super golf swing should *feel;* how your backswing should *feel;* how your grip should *feel;* how impact should feel; how your knees should *feel*. I will teach you how to visualize a successful shot before you address the ball, and then how to translate that visualization into the "feel," or sensitivity of "touch," needed to make the shot you've visualized actually take place.

Let's assume that you are standing on the tee of a par-4 hole. Your sense of sight tells you that the hole bends slightly to the left around some trees. You may feel a slight right-to-left breeze, and you may see the trees blowing with the wind. The fairway may slope a bit from right to left.

Once you have learned to play by feel, you will subconsciously "feed" all of this information into that "computer" inside your skull *(Illustration 1).* You will "program" yourself for the shot. Then you will "push a button" and the visualization of the proper flight of the ball will flash into your mind's eye. Then you will push another button and suddenly you will "feel" a preview of how your swing will feel when you execute the intended shot. Finally, your "computer" will *automatically* move your hands and arms and legs and body in just the right way to make the shot you intended. Your swing and your striking of the ball will feel just as you had imagined they would.

Sound difficult? It really isn't. Given a clear track, the human mind and nervous system can perform amazing feats of coordination. You don't need to "tell" your body what to do, where to move, into what position. In fact, this sort of mental direction merely clutters up the computer of your mind and keeps it from functioning smoothly. The golfer who stands over the ball for half a minute is merely feeding his mind a lot of extraneous information — "keep your head down," "hold on tight at the top," "hit with your left knee" — that it doesn't need. Ask almost any star golfer what he thinks about when he's over the ball and he'll tell you he's imagining how the shot will look, or feel. Or possibly he's thinking about one "key move" that will help create the feel he wants. He trusts his subconscious to take over from there *(Illustrations 2a and 2b).*

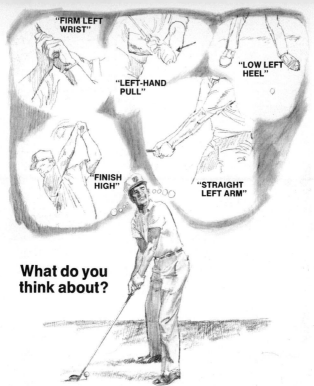

What do you think about?

(Illustration 2a) The average golfer has too many things on his mind as he prepares to make his shot. The more conscious thoughts you have, the greater the chance that you will make an over-controlled, inhibited swing. Conscious thought usually reduces distance and accuracy.

How does your sensory system do it? How does it produce time after time the proper reaction you need to make the shot you have imagined. I say, "who cares?" When I drive my car to the club, I'm vaguely aware that a lot of different mechanical things are happening under the hood. But all I'm really concerned about is steering the vehicle in the proper direction so that it gets me where I want to go and doesn't run into anything along the

What the expert thinks about

(Illustration 2b) Top golfers strive to occupy the mind with only one thought. Often it is how the swing should feel to make the shot visualized beforehand. With your conscious mind free from a variety of thoughts, there is less chance for mental conflict. The subconscious is relatively free to produce an uninhibited swing.

way. That's how it is in golf. All I try to do is steer my mind in the proper direction — by visualizing the shot and imagining how my swing will feel. I'm not one bit concerned about how my sensory system puts it all together.

I do know, however, that one way we program ourselves to produce proper golf swings is by experiencing, again and again, reaction to successful shots. When I strike a putt solidly and *feel* the ball coming off the face and *see* it rolling true to the hole, I am, in fact, sending sensations of feel and sight into my computer. The next time I have a similar putt, my computer will recall for me these same sensations. I will imagine how the putt should feel and look. Then my mind and nervous system will make me move my muscles in a way that produces a putt that actually looks and feels just like I'd intended it should.

The more successful golf shots we experience, the easier it becomes to reproduce them. The more we feel, say, proper hand action during impact, the more readily we will be able to duplicate such movement subconsciously. The more times you watch the flight of successful shots, and relate that sight to the feel of your swing and the club striking the ball squarely, the better you will be able to duplicate such a shot in the future by merely summoning forth the corresponding feel. Never turn your back on successful shots. Watch the ball until it stops rolling.

Can a novice golfer learn the sensation — the feel and sight — of successful shots? How does a 25-handicap player build a "success pattern" of solid driving when he only hits one or two solid drives in a whole month of play? The answer is that he can build "success patterns" in his computerlike mind only if he learns golf the way I teach it — *from the green to the tee.*

Anyone can experience the feel of solid contact and see successful results on two-foot putts. And that's exactly where I think golf should first be learned — from two feet away. That's where I will start to teach you to play by feel.

You may find it necessary to putt from this distance for only five or 10 minutes before progressing to longer putts, short approach shots and, eventually, the full swing. But if you follow my prescription, you won't move on to a longer shot until you have experienced, with reasonable frequency, the *feel* of success with shorter shots *(Illustration 3)*.

Should you falter along the way and lose the feel of, say, a full 5-iron shot, I will ask you to step backward in your training and re-establish a success pattern with a shorter iron.

As director of golf at Palmetto Dunes resort on Hilton Head Island, S.C., and at other locations, I teach golf an average of at least seven hours a day, every work day, and I've taught at this pace for many years. I've given close to 40,000 hours of lessons to people of varying ages, sizes, shapes and, more important, psychological behavior patterns. Also, I think you will come to realize as you read this book that I have a very inquiring mind. During my 38 years in golf — I started as a shop boy when I was five — I've probably done as much thinking about, asking about, trying out and teaching of the golf swing as any other human being. I don't mean to brag, but I do want you to understand that I speak with authority when I tell you that you can learn to play by my "Touch System," and that you will be a much better golfer if you master this method.

Here are some reasons why I know that golf is largely a game that is best played through full use of one's sensory mechanisms:

1. *Most top golfers play primarily by feel.* True, all of them went through a long period of learning mechanics. On occasion, most of them still polish up on their fundamentals by practicing. But, once on the course, the really good players concern themselves primarily with picturing the shot they need and summoning forth the swing "feel" that will produce that shot.

2. *Playing by feel helps produce a dependable, repeating swing.* Effective timing is something that can leave a golfer very quickly. Even a good player can lose his rhythm and timing under pressure. Or his ego might get in his way; he might start a

round playing well within himself, hit some good shots, and then get the notion that he can really let it out. Bingo, he's suddenly jumping at the ball and wondering why he's lost his consistency. A poor player can't be consistent because he's never experienced, or been taught, the feeling of good timing and rhythm. I believe that every golfer has a basic rhythm or pace that is inherent to his or her particular swing. Once a player learns to *feel* this rhythm, and once he learns to bring forth this feel on shot after shot, then he has a consistency factor that will help him produce the same good shots over and over.

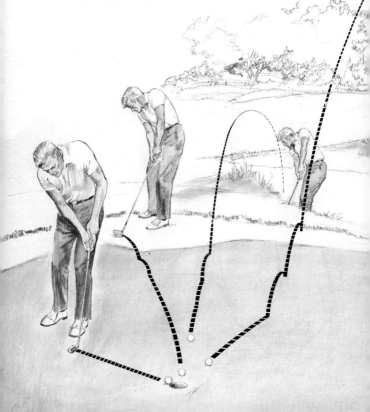

Building success patterns

(Illustration 3) To play by feel, you must first feed your subconscious the sensations—touch and sight—of making successful shots. Then later you can recall the feel and sight of past successful shots as you execute strokes on the course. The way to build success patterns is to start with the easiest shots— putts—and then progress out to chip shots, pitch shots, full iron shots, and, finally, drives. If you falter along the way, you should return to an easier shot, re-establish a success pattern for that shot, and then progress onward to the more difficult shot.

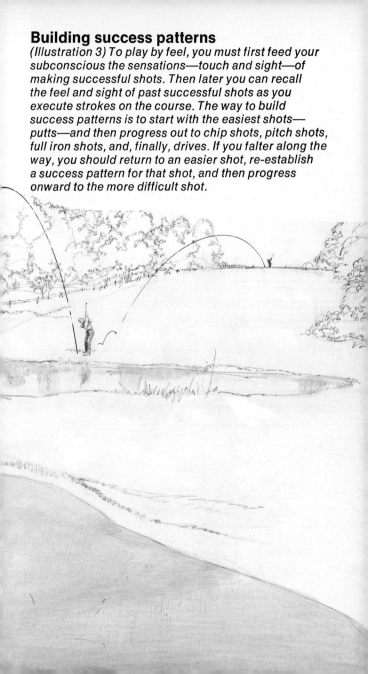

3. *Playing by feel adds distance and accuracy to your shots.* One thing that always seems to amaze spectators at a pro tournament is the great distances that players drive with so little apparent phyical effort. "Look at that Boros," they'll say. "He hits it 50 yards farther than I can, and all the time he looks like he's falling asleep." The pros hit shots farther and straighter than you do, and probably with less effort, for several reasons. But the main reason, when all is said and done, is simply that these players have learned to time their swing to the nth degree. It is this fantastic timing, which is nothing more than fine coordination, that enables them to hit their shots more solidly and with superior clubhead speed.

But even these golfers could not achieve such a fine degree of timing, such outstanding coordination of moving parts, if their minds were cluttered with several different thoughts while they were swinging. No way!

Conscious thought detracts from instinctive action. If you have your mechanics of grip, stance and posture in order, all you need to do before and during your swing is to sense how your swing should feel to strike the ball forward toward the target. This freedom from specific thoughts, such as "head still," "left arm straight," gives your nerves and muscles full rein to carry out the mission that you assigned them when you decided on the pattern of the shot. Never mind if you sway a bit on your backswing, or if you loosen your grip a little at the top, if your computer is working without interference it will automatically correct these mistakes and put everything in order by the time your clubhead reaches the ball. Your sensory system will time your swing better — and you will hit the ball farther and straighter as a result.

Now, let's be realistic about learning to play golf by the "touch system." This approach can work wonders for your game, but only if you follow closely and *practice* the instruction I'll give you in this book. There are no quick tips to instant success in what follows. What there is, however, is a logical approach — a "game plan" for the golfer who is serious about improving. And when I say "improving," I'm talking about at least cutting your current handicap in half.

First I'm going to give you some concepts about the golf swing and the game in general. I suspect that I will change some of your attitudes and, hopefully, will erase any misconceptions you might now have. If nothing else, I want to make you appreciate that it doesn't really take much effort for a 150-pound man, or even a 100-pound woman, to drive a 1.62-ounce ball with a 14-ounce club. More on that later.

Next I will give you a specific program of development so that you can build a success pattern of solid shots.

Then I will describe in great detail how the proper golf swing should look, and how it should feel.

Finally I will touch on various "management techniques" that you can use to produce lower scores on the course, once you have learned to play by feel.

I hope you will trust my method. I know that if you are willing to work at it, you will play much better golf much more consistently. You will do so with much less effort, and with much more enjoyment.

Isn't that what the game is all about?

CHAPTER TWO

PUT YOUR GAME INTO PERSPECTIVE

I'm sure you've seen it happen at the driving range. A young man comes up with his girl friend and suddenly it looks like the Fourth of July. He's trying to impress her with how far he can hit the ball, and he's firing shots in all directions, at all angles. What he doesn't do is hit very many shots very far.

I like to set up next to this type of player, make a nice smooth swing and hit it out there several yards past his best shot. I'll do this for 10 or 15 minutes. By then he'll be looking over at me, wondering what it's all about. Finally, I'll introduce myself and we'll start chatting about the golf swing.

I've done this many times just to prove a point. I want to educate people that there is absolutely no way to successfully "overpower" a golf ball. Trying to force your strength in golf works against you. You actually lose distance.

In this chapter, before we start talking about how to play golf by feel, I want to clear up any misunderstanding you might have about what makes a golf ball go far and straight. I'd just be wasting your time if I taught you how to swing without first explaining the factors that produce distance — and those that reduce it. I find that pupils who lack this understanding almost always go for extra distance by using methods that actually reduce length, and accuracy too. So let's make sure that you have the *mental* understanding needed to properly apply the *physical* instruction that will come later. I really feel that your *attitude* toward your swing determines, to a large extent, how you actually swing.

The first thing you should understand is that you don't have to be very strong, or very big, to hit a golf ball a long way. If strength and size are so important, then how can a person like me, who weighs only 135 pounds, drive the ball 275 yards?

Obviously sheer strength isn't all that vital. Sure, I may weigh only 135 pounds, but the club I'm swinging weighs only about 14 ounces. The ball I'm striking weighs less than two ounces. Now how much strength does it take for a 135-pound man to swing a 14-ounce golf club and hit a 1.62-ounce golf ball *(Illustration 4)*?

Most golfers have trouble with their swing because they fail to look at it in terms of these figures. Subconsciously they seem to think that the ball is much heavier than it really is. They feel that it takes all the strength they can muster to hit it a long way. This is not true. It takes a good sense of rhythm — which most people have. It takes a good sense of coordination or timing — which most people can develop. It helps to be agile and supple. But it does not take as much strength, as much sheer muscle power, as most golfers seem to think. Sure, strength can help, but only if it is properly applied. Usually it isn't.

From now on I would like you to quit relating your strength to the distance you hit your golf shots. Never again feel that you must hit the ball "hard" to make it go far. Remember that the ball weighs very little indeed. Many of my pupils make a much better swing — and actually hit the ball farther — if they imagine that it's a ping-pong ball or, better yet, a bubble. How hard do you have to swing at a bubble?

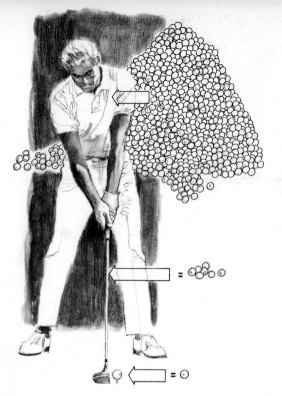

Why swing so hard?
(Illustration 4) A 150-pound golfer weighs about 170 times as much as the club he's swinging—and about 1,480 times as much as the ball he's striking. Most players fail to fully use this tremendous weight and size advantage because they don't realize, subconsciously, just how light the ball really is. They lose distance because they swing with more effort than they need, and thus ruin their timing. They swing AT the ball rather than THROUGH it.

Basically, what it takes to make a golf ball leave its resting place and move forward is energy. The more energy the clubhead imparts to the ball, the farther the ball will go. But you should not equate energy with strength. That's what too many golfers do. And that's why they tense their arms and shoulders, and squeeze the club, and throw themselves off-balance, and mis-hit the ball — and seldom drive nearly as far as they could if they correctly used only a fraction of their strength.

Instead of relating distance to strength, I want you to begin thinking about adding distance through increased clubhead speed and more-solid contact between clubface and ball.

Here is why clubhead speed and solid contact are important. The type of energy you need to drive a golf ball is called *kinetic* energy, the energy of movement. This is the opposite of *potential* energy, often called the "energy of position." After you lift a rock, you've given it *potential* energy. If you drop the rock, the *potential* energy becomes *kinetic* energy as it falls — you'll feel that energy if it lands on your toe. If you stretch a rubber band, you produce *potential* energy. Release the rubber band and you have *kinetic* energy so long as the band keeps moving.

Make your backswing in golf and you produce *potential* energy. During the downswing this energy becomes *kinetic* — moving energy — which is imparted to the ball. The more *kinetic* energy you impart to the ball, the farther it will go.

What is this kinetic energy? Let's look at its formula:

$$E = \frac{MV^2}{2} \quad \textit{(Energy equals one-half of Mass times Velocity squared)}$$

This formula tells us that "velocity" — since it is "squared" in the formula — is the major factor in producing energy. Thus clubhead speed, the "velocity" factor in golf, is vital in producing long drives *(Illustration 5)*.

But "mass" — the clubhead itself — is also a factor. To get full value from the mass of the clubhead, you must strike the ball squarely with it. Strike the ball on the toe or heel of the clubface and you reduce its effective mass *(Illustration 6)*.

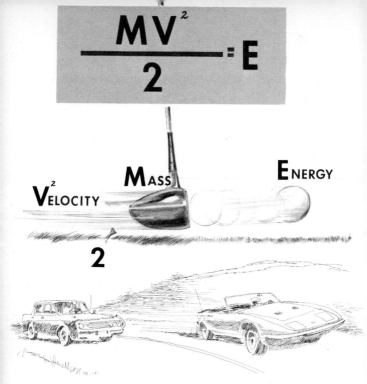

$$\frac{MV^2}{2} = E$$

VELOCITY^2 **M**ASS **E**NERGY

2

Formula for long drives

(Illustration 5) Clubhead speed (velocity) is the main source of distance on shots. Maximum clubhead speed results from a full build-up of potential energy on the backswing and a free release of that energy into the ball with a smooth and well-timed downswing. Imagine your clubhead as being a fast-accelerating sports car, rather than a compact sedan. A secondary factor of distance is the mass of the clubhead itself. Full application of this mass to the ball occurs only when your clubhead strikes it squarely.

Strike it a glancing blow and you do the same. And it doesn't pay to greatly increase the mass factor by adding weight to the clubhead because this additional weight tends to reduce velocity.

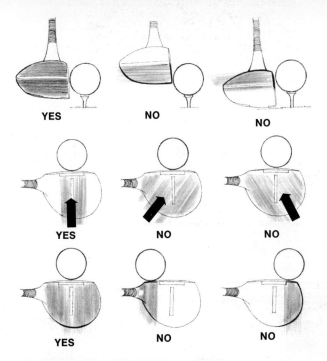

YES NO NO

YES NO NO

YES NO NO

Get the most from your 'mass'

(Illustration 6) On most golf shots, players fail to benefit fully from the weight of the clubhead, which is the mass factor in the transfer of energy to the ball. Whenever the clubhead meets the ball with a glancing or off-center blow, the mass factor is lessened and the player fails to realize his distance potential. Ideal impact finds the clubhead moving along the target line at ball level.

To "see" the relationship between mass and velocity, here is an experiment you can try. Set a golf tee upside-down on the palm of your hand. Make a fist with your other hand and "punch" the tee as far as you can off your palm. Now, replace the tee in your palm and this time merely flick it away as far as you can with the middle finger of your other hand. See — it flies much farther! Why? Because of increased velocity. You can flick your finger much faster than you can move your fist.

There is a valid comparison between flicking the tee with your finger and striking a golf ball with your clubhead. Sure, the tee is much lighter than the ball — I'd hate to flick a golf ball that hard with my finger — but remember, too, that your clubhead is more or less proportionately heavier than your finger. In each instance it is largely the extreme velocity that makes the object shoot forward. *You can lunge your whole body (mass) at the ball in a maximum show of brute strength, but you will never hit the shot as far as you will with a smooth, rhythmical, well-timed, in-balance, well-controlled swing that emphasizes speed of clubhead movement and solid contact.*

What all this means is that you will progress much faster in golf — you will hit the ball much farther and much straighter — if you forget about hitting the ball hard, and, instead, seek other ways to produce clubhead speed (velocity) and solid contact (mass).

I believe that every golfer has a certain basic rhythm. You may have one rhythm; I have another. Our minds and bodies are "mechanized" to a certain pace of life, a certain degree of agility and speed. We should always try to swing the club within the limits of our own basic rhythm. When we do, we swing in balance, and we coordinate ("time") our moving parts well. It's then that we make solid contact with maximum clubhead speed.

Why do most golfers strike the ball more solidly and with greater clubhead speed on shots with the wind than on shots against the wind? Why do players usually make better contact on drives from elevated tees than when the tee is lower than the fairway? It's simply that when you are hitting downwind or from an elevated tee you sense less need to "force" or "muscle" the shot. Your subconscious tells you that the wind, or the elevation of the tee, will give you plenty of distance without any extra effort on your part.

Trying to overpower the ball on golf shots not only forces you beyond your basic rhythm pattern, but it also creates muscular tension. There is absolutely no doubt in my mind that tension is one thing that keeps golfers from hitting shots far and straight. It's really fantastic how tension can slow down your clubhead. Try this trick to see what I mean:

Shake your hand as fast as you can, as if you were trying to flick water from your fingers. Be sure that your arm and wrist are completely relaxed and "loose" as you flick your fingers. Your fingers should click against each other. They should move so fast that they blur together. It's easy so long as your wrist is relaxed.

Now keep on flicking, but gradually tighten your hand and wrist. See how this slows down your movement? Now you can easily distinguish each finger from the others.

This experiment shows how muscular tension can stifle movement. The same sort of thing happens in your golf swing. Tension in the wrong place can reduce your ability to move freely and produce clubhead speed. Muscular tension is one thing that makes short-hitters out of so many golfers.

Now I'd like to warn you about some tension-producing, distance-reducing factors so you'll guard against them as you learn to play golf by feel.

Ironically, perhaps the biggest cause of tension is the tremendous emphasis we put on distance itself. Sit around the 19th hole, and invariably you'll hear how far so-and-so drove on such-and-such hole. Joe may ask Sam what he used on his approach shot, but what Joe really wants to find out is who hit the longer tee shot, or who bangs his irons the farthest. Almost all of us have a distance fetish. That's why most people at a driving range or on a practice tee spend more time with the driver than all their other clubs combined. Power! In golf, as in baseball, everyone wants to hit home runs. And that's why most golfers "strike out."

I'm not all that impressed with power in golf. You shouldn't be either. I've seen very few golfers who know how to handle power. Nicklaus? Sure. But even he swings with only about 80 per cent of his available power. And when you hear talk about the great players, how often is it mentioned how far they hit off the tee? Hogan? I've never heard anyone talk about how far Hogan hit a golf ball. Nelson? Jones? Vardon? Hagen? Sarazen?

What do you think is the average length of drives on the men's pro tour? According to IBM statistics the leading 80 players in 1967-69 averaged only 256 yards off the tee. Yet, everyone seems to think of the pros in terms of 275-300 yard drives. Sure, these men may drive 40 or 50 yards farther than you do, but they are competing on courses that are playing probably 500-1,000 yards longer than yours. Obviously, length off the tee isn't the only reason why they shoot in the 60's so often.

Yet, when the average golfer steps up to his drive, he thinks — he *knows* — that he's expected to hit that ball a very long way. He knows he'll be praised by his friends if he does. He knows that if he fails, he'll seem less a man than those who hit it farther. Sure, a long drive is good for the ego. But must it be a golfer's primary expression of masculinity?

It's all so silly because the more that most players worry about distance, the more tension they create. And, as we've shown, this tension reduces velocity, and thus distance. Tension also destroys timing so that you can't fully turn into kinetic energy all the potential energy you've built up during your backswing. I've noticed that many women golfers, who feel they lack strength, tend to become "lifters." They try to overpower the ball by lifting their arms and head and shoulders into very long and high backswings. From there they become droppers of the club, or pushers of the club. They would build up much more clubhead speed — with much less effort — if they'd coordinate their legs and body with their arms in a true swinging motion.

In the great quest for distance off the tee, most golfers fail to realize the importance of striking the ball squarely. They think they can hit the ball hard *and* square. Most times they do neither. The ball doesn't go far, and it doesn't go straight, because they've swung too "hard."

Not only to golfers over-stress distance, they under-stress the importance of accuracy. Think back to your last round of golf. Replay that round — or make up a typical round — as best you can in your mind. Now, I want you to take a "15-yard-penalty" every time you hit a shot into some sort of trouble. Move the ball back 15 yards from where it finished, *but drop it in a place that gives you a clear shot.* Don't count any penalty strokes. If you hit a shot out of bounds, simply drop the ball in the middle of the fairway, but 15 yards short of where it left the course. If you hit a shot into water or sand, drop it back 15 yards, but in the fairway. Do the same thing anytime you hit into rough or behind trees.

I often allow my pupils to play this way during their playing lessons. It's amazing how much lower they score — even with the 15-yard penalties — when they don't have to count penalty strokes, or hit out of deep grass or sand, or around trees.

It soon hits home to these pupils, as it will to you, that, in golf, accuracy is vastly more important than distance. I'd bet that the average 90-shooter could cut four or five shots from his score — even

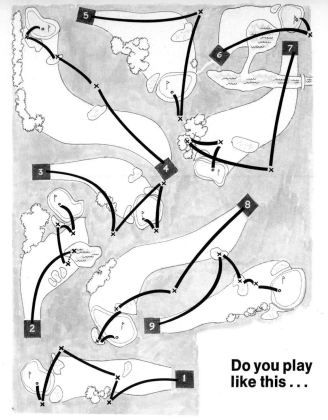

Do you play like this . . .

(Illustration 7a) This is the pattern of play for a golfer who hits long drives, but fails to control his shots. He drives 15 yards farther than his counterpart on the facing page, but usually into trouble. He needs to de-emphasize distance and increase accuracy. Given two putts per green, it has taken him 53 strokes to play this 9-hole course.

sacrificing 15 yards per drive — if he'd *forget distance* and *stress accuracy (see Illustrations 7a and 7b).*

The fantastic thing is that once you quit trying to slug the ball far — once you concentrate on merely making solid contact with a smooth rhythmi-

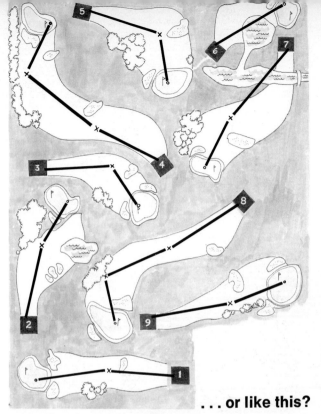

. . . or like this?

(Illustration 7b) This golfer is willing to settle for less distance because he knows it's more important to keep the ball in play. Though his drives are only of average length he still shoots 37—16 shots less than his longer-driving, but wilder, counterpart—for the nine holes. Many golfers actually add distance when they de-emphasize it in favor of merely striking the ball solidly.

cal swing — you'll not only start keeping the ball in play, but you'll actually *add* many of the yards you were seeking when you were trying to slug the cover off the ball. You'll strike the ball squarely more often, and thus get more clubhead (more mass) behind the ball on more of your shots. You will also swing with far less tension and much better coordination, and this will give you greater clubhead speed (more velocity). As you read the later chapters and develop more control of your swing, you will learn to increase *both* distance and accuracy. But it's futile to go for distance before you have control.

I hope by now I've convinced you that trying to hit the ball hard is not the way to hit longer, straighter shots. Now I'd like to tell you about "over-control." This is another tension-producing, distance-reducing disease that you should know about because it afflicts all golfers to some degree.

Over-control in your golf swing is *any action you make that inhibits the natural movement of the clubhead.* Please think about this definition for a moment.

We've talked about one type of over-control, the tendency to try to swing faster than our natural rhythm allows. This forcing the swing in order to add distance usually produces some sort of *action that inhibits the natural movement of the clubhead.*

There are dozens of other causes of over-control, and they all produce some sort of physical inhibition — tightening of your grip, shoving or pushing rather than swinging with your arms, slowing down your leg action *(Illustration 8).*

Every time you over-control your swing, you do so because of some sort of anxiety or fear, conscious or subconscious. Anxiety *must* be present if a player is over-controlling. Eliminate the anxiety and you dispel the tendency to over-control.

For instance, if I hand you an ordinary dime-store water glass, you'll take it from me without a second thought. But what if I tell you, "This glass comes from Tiffany's. It costs $1,000. Whatever you do, don't drop it." Do you think you'll hold that glass in the same relaxed manner? No way! Your fear of dropping the glass will make you *over-*

control it. Put a golfer into a situation where he needs to make a straight drive, or a short putt, to win a tournament, and he's likely to have a similar reaction. He may increase his grip pressure. Over-control.

SHOVING

RESTRICTING SHOULDERS

BLOCKING HIPS

SCOOPING

STIFFENING LEGS

SWAYING FORWARD

Examples of over-control
(Illustration 8) Any action that inhibits the natural free-swinging of your clubhead is likely to cause tension and thus reduce distance. Such inhibitory actions include (clockwise from top-left) shoving with the hands and arms, restricting the backswing shoulder turn, blocking or restricting the downswing hip turn, sliding forward to guide the clubhead through impact, stiffening the legs during the downswing and scooping the clubhead under the ball.

Some golfers fear that they won't get the ball into the air. This fear keeps them from making a smooth swing. They try to shove the clubhead under the ball and scoop it into the air. Over-control.

I drive along in heavy traffic and I look over at the little old lady driving in the next car. She fears she might bump into another car. She's hunched over the steering wheel, holding on with all her might. Over-control.

Beginners get psyched out in golf because the clubface looks so small. They fear they can't return such a small object squarely to the ball. This fear increases when they swing, because the clubhead moves off the line during the backswing. They fear they won't be able to swing it back on line. All of these fears cause all sorts of unnecessary movements that keep a player from making a smooth swing. Over-control.

As the novice golfer gains experience, he begins to realize that the clubface is, indeed, large enough to strike the ball squarely. He learns that he can return the clubhead along the proper line. With this knowledge comes confidence. He loses some of his tendency to over-control. His swing becomes smoother and freer.

Unfortunately, it happens too often that the more experience you gain in golf, the more you start thinking about various *parts* of your swing. You may make a nice, smooth practice swing because all you're doing is loosening up. But then you stand over the ball and think about all the things you should do — and all the things you shouldn't do. You become mentally fearful that you won't do everything just right, which makes you physically tense. By the time you finally get around to moving the clubhead away from the ball, you've primed your subconscious into forcing you to make some sort of over-control.

I can relate back to my own playing career and

recall that I was too "swing conscious" much too long. This caused a certain amount of over-control. Once I'd learned the mechanics of a good swing, I should have stopped thinking in terms of various parts and, instead, begun thinking in terms of the swing as a whole.

Today I know better. I may *practice* to improve a certain part of my swing, but once I'm on the course I relate to the *overall rhythm* of my swing, instead of to the various swing parts. I think about *what* I want to achieve with the shot, rather than *how* to achieve it. I aim the club, visualize how the ball will look in flight, and then merely swing with good rhythm to produce that flight.

If the pro has some great, mystical "secret" that the average golfer lacks, apart from a sound grip and address position, it is his ability to produce a golf swing *that is relatively free from tension and over-control.*

The pro understands the value of what I've told you in this chapter. He knows that he will produce maximum clubhead speed (velocity) and square contact (mass) only if he swings within his basic rhythm and avoids any tendency to over-control the club. He knows that if he tries for extra distance he risks losing the rhythm — and thus the proper timing — of his swing. He keeps at least 10 per cent of his power in his pocket. He knows that fear of failure, or over-concern about various details of his swing, will produce over-controls that inhibit his clubhead speed and keep him from making square contact. The pro doesn't think much about *how* he will swing. He thinks more about *where* he wants the ball to go and *how it will look* going there.

CHAPTER THREE

FIRST STEPS TOWARD BETTER FEEL

At this point in most golf instruction books, the author tells you how to make a 100-per-cent perfect full swing that will drive the ball far and true. That isn't exactly my way of teaching.

Let's look at it this way: Do you strike all your putts squarely? Do they all go more or less the right distance? OK — so you're a great putter. Now, what about your chip shots, your pitch shots? Can you make square contact consistently on the 75-yard approach shots? How about on full 5-iron shots? Are you hitting these shots flush almost every time? Do they fly straight? Is your distance consistent? What about your fairway woods?

I suspect that every reader, regardless of his ability, bogs down somewhere along the line during this progression from putts to full shots. Yet much golf instruction *starts* with telling the pupil how to make a full swing, often with a driver. It tries to teach players to hit long shots in the air before they have learned to hit short shots on the ground. It tries to teach a person to combine the little muscles of his hands and arms with the big muscles of his legs and back in making 200-yard drives before he's even developed any sort of consistency on 20-yard chip shots using *only* his smaller muscles.

In life we learn to crawl and walk before we run.

If we don't, we soon fall down. It's the same in golf. If we try to "run" first by hitting full shots, we "fall down." But then do we go back and learn how to crawl? No. We keep on trying to run. The learning period becomes longer because we keep falling down. That's why golf is so frustrating to so many people.

I've already explained the advantages of playing golf by feel. But to play by feel you must first develop subconscious *patterns* of success. You must impart the feeling of square contact to your own nervous system on shot after shot. You must impart the feeling of smooth rhythm on swing after swing. You must impart a feeling for the length and force of swing needed to make a golf ball go a given distance.

Once you have "fed" these success patterns into your nervous system — once you have "programmed" your computer — you will be ready to play golf by feel. Then you can visualize how a given shot must fly and/or roll if it is to be successful, and merely summon forth the feel you need to actually make that shot successful.

But you cannot expect to build these necessary patterns by hitting full shots. That's like trying to "run" too soon. You'll fall down. And falling down is *not* the success pattern we seek. Hitting a bad shot creates a failure pattern.

The only way to build certain success patterns in golf is to start with the easiest shots and progress from there. For a novice, the easiest shot on which to make square contact is a two-foot putt. That's his starting point. Once he's developed the necessary success patterns on two-foot putts, he moves on to longer putts, then chip shots from off the edge of the green, pitch shots, full short-iron shots, full middle-iron shots, and then either full long-iron or full-wood shots, whichever is easiest.

If somewhere along the line you start hitting bad shots — building failure patterns — you must go

Step 1—Visualize success

(Illustration 9) Start with short putts to develop proper "feel" habits for all shots. First, visualize yourself making the putt. With training, you will master the ability to produce such imagery in your mind's eye. Note: though head positioning of man putting is correct for this right-to-left breaking putt, if putt were straight-in or left-to-right, his head would be turning more "under" and less "around."

back a step or two to an easier shot. And you must stay at that level until you re-establish your success patterns.

I will guide you along the way. I will tell you *what* you should feel and *what* you should see. I'll help you make sure that you feed your nervous system success patterns, not failure patterns.

I know from experience that this method of learning is the best for both beginners and experienced golfers. It reduces confusion, and that builds confidence. Because this system starts with the relatively *simple* movement of the putting stroke, in the end it will give you a *simpler* golf swing. I mean a swing that is free from needless movements that can cause errors.

Because this system starts with putts and short shots, it forces you to learn the importance of control. Distance will come in time, but I'm not going to let you "go for the fences" until you learn control.

Because this system of learning is based on feel, it largely eliminates the problem of overthinking — "paralysis from analysis" — that inhibits so many golfers. The system also provides an orderly progression of learning — from putts, to chips, to irons, to woods — that gives you a sound base on which to build a *lasting* swing.

And, finally, this system allows you to progress at whatever rate of speed your talent and your degree of application allow. Obviously, the player who can practice daily will usually move ahead faster than one who practices once a week. The more-experienced golfer may need to spend only minutes in building success patterns of putting before he moves on to chipping. The beginner may take hours. Some advanced golfers may even choose to start with full iron shots, bypassing the putting and short-iron segments. This might work in some cases, but I suggest you spend at least a few minutes re-establishing success patterns on short shots before you attempt full shots. I think the reasons for your starting with short putts will become more obvious as you read on.

You are now ready to take your first steps in learning to play golf by feel. The best place to do this is on the putting green at your course. You'll need your putter and a half-dozen or so balls.

Take your normal putting grip *(Illustration 10).* I would like you to check to see that:

1.   The back of your left hand and the palm of your right hand are facing in the same direction that your putterface is looking.

2.   That your left-hand fingers, if extended when you're in position to putt, point almost straight down, vertically, to the ground.

If your normal grip does not meet these two requirements, adjust it now so that it does. In making sure your left-hand fingers point almost straight down, don't arch your wrists until they feel tense. Merely make sure you don't allow any inward bending at the base of your left thumb. Address the ball in closer to your feet and raise your hands until any such cupping disappears. Your left wrist should feel "high."

The principle of having your palms facing each other and aligned with the clubface is basic to proper gripping on *all* normal golf shots, from putts to drives. If your present grip for fairway and tee shots doesn't produce this effect, I strongly urge that you make it conform.

The idea of the "high" left wrist also applies to non-putts, though to a slightly lesser degree since you play the ball farther from your feet on longer shots.

By putting your hands into a palms-facing position that aligns with the clubface, and by taking any slack out of the top of your wrists, you will help avoid turning or rolling your hands to the right or the left during your putting stroke. You're in a position to move your hands straight back and

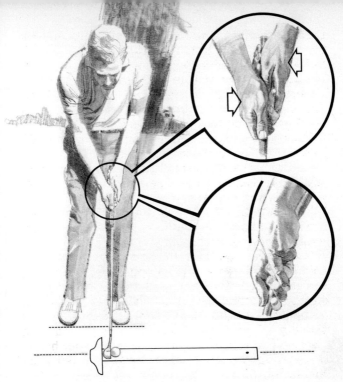

Step 2—Set up correctly

(Illustration 10) Master the simple mechanics of grip and set-up on short putts. Palms must be facing, and wrists sufficiently raised to produce a pendulum-like stroke. Putterface should "square" with intended line at address.

straight through like a pendulum, without opening or closing the putterface.

When I think back to the old players, I recall that many of them held their wrists very low. That's why they would often roll their wrists, and pull or push their putts, under pressure. Horton Smith was an outstanding exception. But look at the great putters of today; they all set their hands relatively high.

Having your hands in good position is very important, but so is holding the club with the right amount of pressure, and that goes for all shots with every club. As I see it, there are three broad categories of grip pressure. You can use a *loose* grip, a *light* grip, or a *tight* grip.

A loose grip doesn't give you enough control. The club slips in your hands.

A tight grip produces over-control. It causes tension which reduces motion. (Remember how we lost movement and hand speed when we gradually tightened our wrist as we flicked our fingers.) Many times a golfer will hold the club too loosely, lose control, and then grab hold too tightly, all in the same swing. That's like slamming on the brakes of your car. You lose velocity (distance) and you also lose a large amount of feel.

The ideal grip pressure is *light.* By "light," I mean a grip that gives you just enough pressure to control the club — to keep it from slipping — but not so much that you will over-control it. A light grip gives you control, maximum feel, and allows a great deal of freedom of motion. Obviously you need a firmer grip on a full shot than on a two-foot putt. But on any shot the correct pressure is simply light enough to control the club in your hands without sacrificing any degree of feel or freedom of movement during your swing.

Now, let's talk generally about what we want to accomplish with our putting stroke. First, we want it to be simple. I once saw a magazine article that showed several different golfers at impact on full shots. I believe they called it "the moment of truth." All of these players looked about the same when they were actually striking the ball, but they all made a great many different moves beforehand. It was really fantastic to see the different angles and positions through which these players moved the club before they swung it back "square" to the target line.

I don't think that all these moves are necessary. The ideal swing puts the player into proper impact position without a lot of fuss along the way. So when you are putting, don't try to push the club outside the line or inside the line. Don't try to open the clubface or close the clubface. Merely swing the clubhead away from the ball and into a position from where you can return it squarely to the ball with the least chance of error. If you develop an uncomplicated putting stroke, you'll carry the same simplicity into your fuller swings with the longer clubs.

Think of a child's playground swing as it goes back and forth, back and forth. It goes up and back and comes down and forward along the same line. At the bottom of its arc, it always passes over the grass at the same height. It's a simple back-and-forth movement. The golf swing isn't exactly similar, but the pendulum movement of the playground swing does exemplify the rhythmical simplicity of movement that you should seek as you practice your putting *(Illustration 11)*. A simple putting stroke is more likely to produce square contact than will a complex stroke with a lot of hand and wrist movement and a lot of pushing and shoving. The same principle holds true on all other shots in golf as well.

With this simplicity of movement in mind, I'd like you to drop your golf balls about two feet out from the hole, hold the club as I've described and begin trying to sink as many of these putts as you can.

You'll find it easier to swing like a pendulum if you place your feet so that an imaginary line across your toes is parallel to the line of your putt. This is called the "square" stance because a line across your toes would form a 90-degree — or "square" — angle with your putterface.

In trying to hole each putt, you must first visualize the line that you think the ball must follow.

41

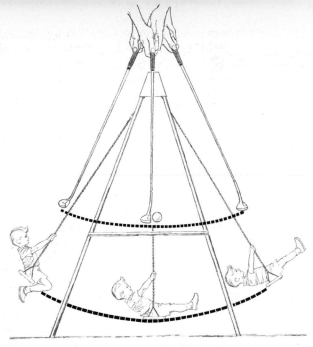

Step 3—Accelerate putterhead

(Illustration 11) Execute putting stroke in a manner similar to the back and forward motion of a child's playground swing. Make certain, however, that putterhead accelerates through the ball.

Never allow yourself to make a putt until you "see," or "sense," this line (Illustration 9). If you can't see it at first, actually draw the line on the green. Use a pocket knife or a golf tee. Don't tear up the green — keep the cut shallow and light.

Later, as you move out from the hole on longer putts, this imaginary line that you visualize may necessarily curve somewhat to allow for any curving of the putt due to sidehill slants of the green. You'll learn how to read the proper curve on sidehill putts as you gain experience, but even if you're a beginner and it seems you never quite select the right amount of break, you still should always "see" some sort of intended line before you putt.

I think that every golfer, even with just a limited amount of experience, can develop the ability to properly "read" most putts. But I'm equally convinced that many golfers — maybe most — waste this skill by failing to visualize beforehand the path that their putt will take. Many players do look at the putt and come to some vague conclusion about which way it will break. But then they set up over the ball *before* they actually see the specific line. This forces them to spend a longer period of time over the ball, and gives their back and wrist muscles a chance to stiffen. Always determine your specific line *before* you address the ball.

"If you don't see the putt line," says Curtis Person, the man who has dominated Senior golf competition the last several years, "I back away and look again. I've got to see the line all the way to the cup, almost like a small valley for my ball to roll down. I mean I've actually got to visualize my ball diving into the cup.

"Once I've got this image in my mind, then it sends me a signal about how hard to stroke the putt. I'm a firm believer that the mind is a computer and it sends a message to the hands.

"How do you hit soft and hard shots with a club? The mind sends the hands a message. It's all mental."

Once you set up over the ball, with the prescribed grip, and a square stance, all you need to do is place the putterface squarely behind the ball, at a right angle to your chosen line, and swing the putterhead back and through along that line *(Illustration 10)*.

It may seem elementary for me to tell you to place your putter squarely behind the ball so that it faces down the target line. This *is* a simple matter, especially if your putter is one of those that has a line across the top of its head at a right angle to the face. But you'd be surprised how many golfers I've seen — par-shooters and better — who carelessly mis-align their putterheads. If these players can mis-align putts, where accuracy is so vastly important, imagine how this same careless tendency might carry over into full shots with the longer clubs.

It is also vital that you develop the habit of striking the ball with the same part of the putter-face each time. Failure to do so will make putts that are struck with exactly the same force vary up to several feet in the distance they travel. An off-center strike on a 15-foot putt can make the ball finish two or three feet short of the hole.

Please remember above all else that in these practice sessions we are trying to build success patterns. The more times you *feel* a putt struck squarely and the more times you *see* it roll toward

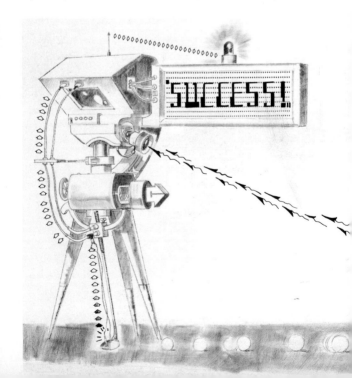

and drop into the hole, the more you reinforce a success pattern *(Illustration 12)*. The more you mis-read a putt or mis-hit a putt, the more you reinforce a failure pattern. The more difficult it becomes to summon forth the proper feel on future putts.

Ideally, on all putts — and on all normal full shots as well — your clubhead should feel like it's accelerating during your forward stroke. You should feel that it's picking up speed gradually as it moves *into* the ball and *through* the ball. *THROUGH* the ball. I know that as you putt your main concern is going to be to strike the ball squarely and knock it into the hole. But never, *never* let yourself lose sight of the fact that you are accelerating the putterhead *through* the ball and *down* the line, instead of merely *at* the ball.

If I could be with you at this moment, I would

Step 4— ### Register success

(Illustration 12) FEEL the accelerating putterhead strike the ball squarely, and SEE the putt roll into the hole. Feed these sensations of success to your "computer" for future reference on similar shots.

hold out my palm and ask you to slap it with your right hand, using about the same movement you'd make during your golf swing. As you swung your hand forward, just as it was about to strike mine, I'd suddenly pull my hand out of the way. Do you think you would continue to swing your hand and arm forward? I'll bet 10-to-1 that you'd put on the brakes and quickly halt your forward movement.

This is "over-control." It happens whenever a golfer swings his clubhead *at* the ball instead of *through* the ball. It doesn't happen when you make a practice swing, because there's no ball to swing "at." It doesn't happen when you make a practice putt. But it does happen to most golfers when they see a little white ball in the way of their clubhead. Something in the human sensory system makes us hit *at* objects. And whenever we hit *at* something the normal subconscious tendency is to slow down our hands and "guide" them toward the object. This tendency seems even stronger when we try to hit an object with another object.

To be a long hitter in golf you must learn to overcome this instinct to swing *at* the ball. You can't guide your club and still hit long shots. The best place to start re-training your subconscious to avoid swinging the clubhead at the ball is on the putting green, always accelerating your putterhead *through* the ball. At first you may stroke the ball far past the hole. When this happens you should lighten your grip and make a shorter backstroke. But always accelerate the putterhead *through* the ball.

Keep practicing these short putts until you can feel the repetitive motion of your arms moving the clubhead back and forward, accelerating into the ball and striking it squarely. You will know when you have not met the ball squarely. You will know when you've failed to swing the clubhead *through* the ball.

Remember to hold the club in the prescribed

position — palms facing, hands high. Remember to visualize your line *before* you set up to the ball. Hold the club light — not loose, not tight. Take a square stance. Swing the clubhead only with your hands and arms, never using your legs or hips or moving your head. Again, we are trying to build a *simple* stroking pattern with a minimum of extraneous movement. *Feel* the acceleration of the clubhead *through* the ball and *down* the line. *Feel* the solid contact. *See* the ball roll into the hole.

These are the success patterns you must instill before you go on to longer putts. Once you've programmed your computer with these patterns on short putts, move on back to six-footers and do the same thing. Then 12-footers and 20-footers. If you find yourself making failure patterns somewhere along the line, then go back to a shorter putt and re-establish your success patterns.

Remember that our goal is to create good habits. I want you to experience the *visual and physical reactions* of *seeing* successful putts and *feeling* successful putts. Then, in the future, you'll be able to re-create success by first visualizing a successful putt, then sensing how a successful putt will feel, then executing that feel.

As I've said, some of you won't need to spend as much time as others on the putting green before moving on to chip shots. But never move on until you feel you've established a true success pattern. If during the process you find that you are getting tired, either mentally or physically, call it quits for that session. If you keep going, you'll only find yourself reinforcing failure patterns.

CHAPTER FOUR

BUILDING FEEL
OFF THE GREEN

Once you've mastered the feel of long putts, it's time to move on to chip shots from just off the green. Start with shots from a foot or so off the edge and gradually move farther and farther away as you develop and strengthen your success patterns.

These shots differ from putts in that, instead of rolling the ball all the way to holes, you now should fly it onto the green before it begins to bounce and roll. Why run the risk of a bad bounce off the irregular fairway surface? Why take a chance on your ball slowing down too quickly in the heavier fringe grass? Play to land your shots on the smoother — and thus truer — putting surface whenever possible.

Too many golfers fail on these short shots because they choose the wrong club. To chip the ball onto the green, you'll need a club that has enough slant or "loft," to its face to get the ball into the air. But *which* club?

Let's say you're just a few feet off the edge of the green and the hole is 30 feet away. You might feel that by using a 3-iron and hitting the ball just onto the green, it will run too far past the hole. A 5-iron shot might pull up short. Then the club to use in this situation is the 4-iron.

The point is that the best club is the *least-lofted*

you can use to carry the ball just onto the smooth surface of the green, without its rolling far past the hole *(Illustration 13)*. The least-lofted club will roll the ball the farthest. Thus you won't need to strike it so hard. You can take a shorter swing with less leg and body movement. With this *simpler* swing, you'll find it much easier to control the movement of the clubhead back and forward through the ball.

Another reason to use the least-lofted club you can under the circumstances is because most people find it easier to judge distance on shots that roll most of the way than on those that fly most of the way.

If I tell a pupil to take the ball and roll it off his fingertips to the hole, he'll make it finish much closer more often than if I tell him to make it fly, say, three-quarters of the way and then bounce and roll to the cup.

Playing chip shots with minimum carry also happens to fit in with my method of teaching people to play by feel. Because there's less difference in loft, it's much easier for my pupils to progress from the putter to a 4- or 5-iron for chipping than to an 8- or 9-iron.

As you move farther and farther back from the green, you'll need to use those more-lofted clubs. Obviously, if you land a 3-iron shot on the green from 50 yards out, your ball may skitter across the putting surface and over the back edge. From that far out you'll need more loft so you can hit the ball high and make it settle gently and stop quickly on the green. But never use more loft than you need. As you gain experience, you will learn how the ball flies with various clubs. You'll soon get the knack of choosing just the right club to produce the type of shot that you've visualized beforehand.

Before you start chipping shots from just off the edge of the green, let's make sure that you are setting up to the ball properly and holding the club correctly. The chip shot is much like the long putt,

THIS is easier than THIS
*(Illustration 13) Most people have
better success rolling an object to a
target than they do lofting it. Thus most
golfers have better success chipping short
shots just onto the smooth putting surface,
and letting the ball bounce and run to the hole,
than they do lofting it most of the way with a pitch shot.*

but it does differ slightly, and you'll need to modify your address position accordingly *(Illustration 14).*

It will help if you realize that the "shape" of your swing must change slightly. On putts your clubhead *swept* over the grass on a fairly level path, hardly raising and lowering at all as you stroked back and through. You swept the ball forward along the ground. But in chipping you'll be playing shots from deeper grass, often with the ball nestled down. If you try to sweep the ball for-

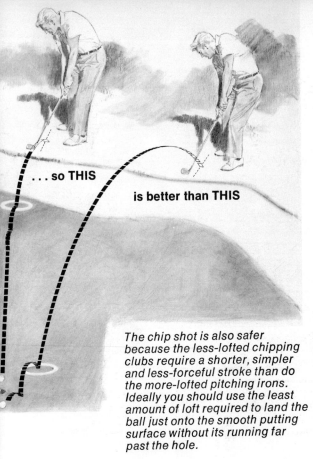

... so THIS

is better than THIS

The chip shot is also safer because the less-lofted chipping clubs require a shorter, simpler and less-forceful stroke than do the more-lofted pitching irons. Ideally you should use the least amount of loft required to land the ball just onto the smooth putting surface without its running far past the hole.

ward with a relatively level, putt-like stroke, your clubhead will probably snag in the grass behind the ball, or it may sweep over the grass but only catch the top part of the ball. Thus you'll need to swing your clubhead somewhat higher going back so that it will return to the ball with a slightly sharper angle of descent than when you were putting.

What we really want on these shots is to make the clubhead swing down and meet that ball just

Variations between putting and chipping

(Illustration 14) A few minor adjustments in address position are necessary when you move from long putts to chip shots from just off the green. In chipping, play the ball an inch or two farther to the right in your stance while keeping your hands in the same place they

an instant *before* it reaches the bottom of its arc. We want to strike the ball with a slightly *down-ward-moving* clubhead. Why? Why not sweep the ball away with the clubhead reaching the bottom of its arc at the exact point when it reaches the ball? Such precise contact is simply too difficult to be practical. Too often when you try to make your clubhead touch down exactly *at* the ball, you will hit *behind* it. You don't leave yourself a big enough margin for error.

When you strike iron shots with a slightly down-

occupied on putts. Also, set up with a bit more weight on your left foot. These alterations will help you avoid hitting behind the ball. Also, choke down on the grip of your chipping club for added control, and pull your left foot back a bit, away from the target line, in an open stance.

ward-moving clubhead, you lessen chances that you'll hit behind the ball. You increase your margin for error. And you don't sacrifice any quality of shot in striking a downward blow because iron clubs are designed to strike the ball while moving slightly downward. The ball will slide and spin up the clubface and then shoot off into the air. The initial angle of trajectory of the ball's flight is determined by the effective loft of the club — the angle of the clubface at that time when the ball leaves it.

Never fear that you won't get the ball into the air if you meet it with a downward-moving clubhead. About the only time you'll have trouble making iron shots fly is when you try to sweep the clubhead *under* the ball. Such attempts usually cause you to either hit behind the ball — a "fat" shot — or to "skull" it by catching the side or top of the ball with the leading edge of the blade on your upswing.

To make sure that you give these chip shots a slightly downward tap, play the ball an inch or two farther right in your stance than you did on putts. But keep your hands forward so that they are in position to *lead* the clubhead through the ball.

You should keep the majority of your weight on your left foot on these short shots. This also helps you to strike the ball before you brush the grass. If you were to set up with your weight on your right foot, or if you shifted it there during your swing, you'd probably hit the shot "fat," striking the turf behind the ball. By keeping your weight on your left foot, you automatically move the lowest part of your swing arc forward, to your left, and thus avoid hitting behind the ball.

On your close-in chip shots you'll be using the less-lofted clubs — 3-iron, 4-iron, 5-iron. Since these clubs are also used on full shots to hit the ball considerable distances, they are constructed with longer shafts than those in your putter and shorter irons. But you don't need all that extra length of shaft on these short shots. So shorten your grip. Choke down a few inches. This shortened grip will give you better control of the club and feel for your swing.

To keep the excess shaft-length from getting in the way of your arms, merely open your stance — pull your left foot back a few inches farther than your right from the target line — so that you are slightly facing the hole. This open stance not only allows the shaft to extend out to your left side, instead of to your middle, but also makes it easier to sight your target and swing the clubhead out toward it on your follow-through.

Thus we see the subtle changes you need to make in going to chip shots: Ball a bit back in stance. Hands forward. Ball a bit farther from feet. Wrists less arched. Weight on left foot. Stance slightly open. Shortened grip on the club. And be sure to use only enough loft to make the ball fly over the fringe and then run to the hole.

These changes in your address position, along with the built-in characteristics of the irons themselves, will automatically give you the proper swing for these short approach shots. Otherwise, you should handle everything just as you did on your putts. That is:

1. *Visualize the shot.* Before you address the ball, be sure to visualize the path it should take as it flies over the fringe and bounces and rolls to the hole. Make a special note as to the spot on the green where you want the shot to touch down.

2. *Grip the club "lightly," with just enough pressure to avoid slippage.* Try to maintain a consistent pressure on the club throughout your stroke. Also, try to keep the pressure between the thumb of your top hand and the palm of your bottom hand constant throughout.

3. *Keep your swing simple.* Don't sway your head or your body back and forth with your arms. As your swing gets longer you will unconsciously start turning your hips and using your legs, *but only in reaction to the wider sweeping of the clubhead.* Let your legs react when they must to preserve your balance and rhythm, but don't force them to act. Don't complicate your action unnecessarily. Continue to picture in your mind the simple backward-forward movement of the child's playground swing.

4. *Accelerate through the ball.* Try tossing the ball side-arm to the hole with your right hand,

holding it gently in your fingertips. *Feel* the acceleration of your arm and hand as they swing forward. Apply the same feeling to your chip shot. But don't force the club forward. Wait for the acceleration. Remember that the ball you're striking weighs less than two ounces. All it needs is a tap. The clubhead swings down, brushes the grass and continues forward. The fact that the ball happens to get in the way is incidental.

5.   *Feel.* Feel the club held lightly in your hands and fingers. Feel it move gently back and forward, brushing the grass. Feel the rhythmical movement of your arms. Feel the crisp contact of the clubhead with the ball. Feel the ball spring forward off the clubface. See the ball fly and land and bounce and roll to the hole. Relish these success patterns of feel and sight. Feed them into your subconscious. Program your computer.

Once you learn to strike the ball squarely and make it finish near the hole with reasonable consistency, move back farther from the green and repeat the process. As you move back, you will need to use a club with a bit more loft, one that will land the ball on the green but make it stop quicker, without running far past the hole.

Because you are hitting a longer shot with a club that provides less roll, you'll need a longer swing with a bit more acceleration. You'll get this longer swing automatically after a few tries if you continue to visualize your intended shot pattern before you address the ball. You also should find that your legs and lower body automatically enter into your swing more and more as it gets longer. Blend their movement with the motion of your arms and shoulders. Make your swing a coordinated back and forward movement. Keep your movement simple and smooth. Remember the playground swing.

Are you still striking the ball with a downward-moving clubhead? Good. As your swing gets longer and longer, you'll find that your clubhead actually starts cutting into the turf, taking a divot. If you're striking the ball as you should — before reaching the bottom of your swing arc — the divot mark should appear *in front* of the ball's original position.

As you progress to longer shots, you'll find it more and more difficult to make the ball finish close to the hole. This is normal. As your swing gets longer, you'll bring more and more muscles into play. Your chance for error will increase. The longer the shot, the longer you must practice it to arrive at the desired patterns of success. If you find it impossible to achieve success from a certain distance, merely move closer to the green and work on shorter pitch shots, or chip shots, until you re-establish a success pattern. Then try again on the longer shot.

FIND YOUR FULL-SWING RHYTHM

Another thing you'll notice when you try longer shots is the temptation to hit the ball "hard." You'll find yourself, almost subconsciously, beginning to swing with more force than you really need. In short, you'll be tempted to forsake the basic swing rhythm that you established on the putting green. You must avoid this temptation at all costs.

As I stressed earlier, everyone has a basic rhythm or pace to his swing. It is very difficult to increase the pace of your swing without sacrificing control of the club. Swing too hard and you'll mis-hit the shot. You won't get the full *mass* of the clubhead into the ball.

Also, forcing your swing ruins your timing, the coordination of your moving parts. Poor timing causes a loss of clubhead speed before it reaches the ball. You'll waste your kinetic power. Also, you'll over-use your arms and neglect the big muscles of your back and legs.

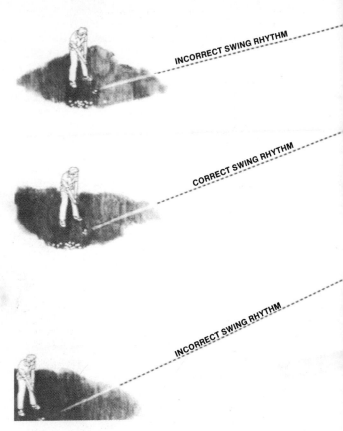

INCORRECT SWING RHYTHM

CORRECT SWING RHYTHM

INCORRECT SWING RHYTHM

You will know when you're losing control. Your shots won't feel squarely struck. Your shots won't finish near the target. They won't fly on a relatively consistent trajectory. Swinging the club will feel like hard work.

At this point you must cut back 10 per cent and "put it in your pocket." You must put your priority on making square contact with an accelerating clubhead that's moving through the ball. *The best way to develop distance in golf is to first develop*

Take 2, 3, 5—even ten strokes off your golf score.

You get it all and much, much more every month in Golf Digest.

Thousands of Golf Digest's readers are actually lowering their handicaps by this much or more by following the expert instruction they receive every month in Golf Digest . . . combining practice with detailed lessons by the world's best playing and teaching professionals.

And Golf Digest's outstanding instruction is complimented by colorful features that cover the whole golfing scene . . . from the latest in equipment to the world's most beautiful and challenging courses.

Business Reply Mail

NO POSTAGE NECESSARY IF MAILED IN THE UNITED STATES

POSTAGE WILL BE PAID BY

Golf Digest

SUBSCRIPTION DEPARTMENT
1255 PORTLAND PLACE
BOULDER, COLORADO 80302

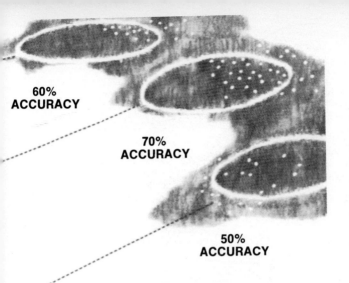

60% ACCURACY

70% ACCURACY

50% ACCURACY

Find your basic rhythm

(Illustration 15) After you have developed success patterns on putts, chips and pitch shots, select a target area of about 15 paces in diameter. First, hit 50-100 shots to this target with your most-lofted club, using a very relaxed, easy swing. Note what percentage of your shots finish in the target area. Repeat the process from 10, 20, maybe 30, yards farther out, but with the same club. Again, figure the percentages of successful shots. Note at which distance you are most accurate. The swing rhythm used at that distance is the rhythm you should feel you are using on all full shots with any club.

a basic rhythm that allows you to make square contact with a well-timed swing.

Sooner or later, as you move farther back from the green, you will reach the point where you are finally making a full swing with your most-lofted club. At this point in your development I'd like you to establish the basic rhythm you will then use on all of your normal full shots.

I'd like you to go to your club's practice green or a secluded area of fairway. Select a target that's in the center of a circle about 15 paces in diameter. Step back whatever distance from the target you feel you will hit the ball if you use a very relaxed swing with the most-lofted club in your bag.

Hit 50 to 100 balls to this target using a very "easy," yet full, swing. See how many of your shots finish in that circle. Next move back 10 yards and repeat the process with the same number of balls. Obviously, the extra length of the shot will require that you make a more forceful swing. See how many of these shots finish in the circle *(Illustration 15).*

If you put more of the shorter shots in the circle, then that "easy" swing you used has the basic rhythm that you should use on *all* normal full shots with your irons.

If you put more balls in the circle with the second batch of balls — from the longer distance, using the more-forceful swing — then this is a better swing rhythm for you to use on all of your iron shots. But go ahead and hit another batch of balls from still another 10 yards farther out. Continue moving back like this until you find the distance — and the swing rhythm — that give you best results. Again, it is this rhythm that you should use on all iron shots. Obviously, it is the rhythm that gives you maximum distance with maximum control.

Some experienced players may try this experiment and find that they have not been using their full energies in swinging. They may find a latent source of power that they actually can control. Most, however, will find that they get maximum control — and a surprisingly large amount of distance — with a swing pace that feels slower and more effortless than the rhythm they had been using. If you are such a player, you must discipline yourself through practice to hit all iron shots at this reduced swing pace.

CHAPTER FIVE
HOW YOUR SWING SHOULD LOOK

Once you reach the point where you are hitting full shots with your most lofted club, and once you've established your basic swing rhythm, you'll find it very helpful to understand the "shape" of a good golf swing. Your concept of how the swing should *look* will directly affect how you interpret my advice — in the next chapter — on how a good swing should *feel*.

Let's suppose you have a big loop at the top of your present swing. On your backswing you move your clubhead around your body on a very low path. It goes well behind your back, but not very high. Then you lift your hands and arms high over your head and chop down on the ball as if it were a piece of kindling.

I could describe to you how it feels to make a proper takeaway, a proper backswing and a proper downswing. This would help you quite a bit. As you applied these sensations of feel to your swing, it would automatically take on a better shape. If your backswing were too "flat," you'd subconsciously make it more upright.

But you will improve the shape of your swing much faster when playing by feel if you understand beforehand what that shape should be. With this shape implanted in your mind, you'll move toward it faster — subconsciously — as I later describe the correct sensations of how it feels.

It is much, much easier to learn the feel of a *simple* swing than it is to learn the feel of a complex swing. In this chapter I'm going to dwell on the shapes of the simple golf swing — the simpler the better. Show me a simple swing, free from excessive motion that has no purpose, and I'll show you an efficient swing, one that produces consistency even under pressure.

As I describe the shape of this efficient swing, I'd rather you *not* try to fit your swing to it. I may ask you to alter your address position slightly, but I don't want you to get bogged down in making all kinds of new moves. All I want at this point is for you to understand how a good swing looks. Once you have this understanding, you'll be ready to go ahead and learn to swing by feel. Then the shape of your swing will automatically fall into place.

First, I'd like you to understand how your golf swing should appear if you were to view it while looking down the line to the target.

If you watched yourself hit balls from this vantage point, you'd soon realize one important fact: You never hit the shot straight if your clubhead isn't *moving along the target line* when it strikes the ball. It's impossible to hit a shot straight if your clubhead moves outside the target line during its forward swing, either before or after it contacts the ball. This is perhaps the most important thing for you to know about the shape of the golf swing *(Illustration 16).*

Thus our ideal golf swing begins to take shape, with the clubhead moving *along* — never across — the target line.

It also makes sense to me that the greater the distance the clubhead moves more or less along the target line, the better the chance that it will be moving close to that line when it meets the ball. If you swing your clubhead more or less on line for

How the clubhead path affects your shots

(Illustration 16) Your shots will fly straight toward a target only if your clubhead is moving along the line to that target (dotted line) during impact. If your shots start to the left and then bend to the right (pull-slice), or if they start left and either continue in that direction (pull) or bend farther left (pull-hook), your clubhead must be cutting across the line from outside to inside during impact. If shots start to the right and then hook, push or slice, clubhead must be swinging from inside to outside line.

five inches, you'll hit more shots straight than if you move it near the line for only one or two inches. The pros I talk to are becoming increasingly aware of the value of "extending the flight path"— increasing the distance that their clubhead moves close to the target line.

If the clubhead should move on the line during impact, then where should it move just before and after it travels that line? It is physically impossible to make a good swing without moving the club-head inside the line *on both your backswing and your follow-through.* I feel the ideal clubhead path is *along* the target line during the takeaway, to *inside* the line during the backswing, to *along* the line in the hitting area, and then back to inside the line during the follow-through—along, inside, along, inside.

Some instructors argue that the clubhead should not move straight back from the ball, along the line, during the takeaway. They feel it should move inside the line as soon as it starts back from the ball. It's been my observation over the years that the vast majority of the pros on tour do start the clubhead moving straight back. Some keep it moving on line longer than others — I'd say about 12 inches for Hogan on drives, but maybe only four or five for Snead. But generally they don't move it off the line until they've fully extended their left arm and thus established a "radius" for their swing. Most keep the clubhead moving on line until it has moved back past their right foot.

I've also found, however, that some golfers, especially beginners, strive to keep the clubhead "on line" too far into the backswing. They move it straight back until they sway sideways like a flag-pole in the wind. These players are afraid that if they *turn* themselves away from the ball and let the clubhead move inside the line, they won't get it back on line and returned squarely to the ball. Those who start learning the game on the green with short putts and then gradually work back to longer and longer shots don't develop this fear. They gain confidence about making solid contact — building success patterns — as they progress.

We've now established that the clubhead's path is along-to-inside-to-along-to-inside the target line. Now let's complete the shape of the swing as viewed from this angle. All that remains is to state that at the top of the swing the club itself should

Set your club 'on track'

(Illustration 17) At the top of the backswing, your clubshaft should align more or less parallel with your target line. It should not point across the line to the right, or away from the line to the left. Imagine that your target line forms the right rail, and your clubshaft the left rail, of a set of tracks.

align more or less parallel to the target line.

Ideally, if you could extend the clubshaft indefinitely in the direction it's pointing at the top of your swing, it would never cross the target line. Nor would it angle off far to the left of target. Imagine that your target line is the right rail of a set of railroad tracks. Now, if you could look straight down on yourself, your clubshaft should form the left rail *(Illustration 17)*.

The distance separating these two "rails" is determined by how far you swing your clubhead inside the target line during your backswing. Generally, tall golfers play the ball in closer to their feet than do short golfers. If they didn't, to reach the ball they would need longer-shafted clubs than they could easily control. Thus tall golfers generally have more upright swings. They don't move the clubhead as far inside the line. Their "rails" are closer together.

Golfers like Arnold Palmer and Lee Trevino, who have relatively "flat" swings, move the clubhead much more to the inside than do others like Jack Nicklaus and Al Geiberger, who swing on relatively "upright" swing planes. If you looked down from directly above these men as they swung, the "rails" would be farther apart for Palmer and Trevino than for Nicklaus and Geiberger.

There is no set standard for how far apart your "rails" should be—how flat or upright you should make your swing plane—so long as the rails are more or less parallel when you reach the top of your swing. If you play the ball relatively far away from your feet, you'll probably swing on a relatively flat plane—more "around," instead of "over" your body. Since it's normal to play the ball closer to your feet on a 9-iron shot than on a drive—because the 9-iron is a much shorter club than the driver—you'll automatically make a more upright swing with the 9-iron.

If you take a flat swinger like Trevino and an upright swinger like Nicklaus, and if they both keep their left arms fully extended throughout their backswings, the flat swinger's hands will not move as high as the upright swinger's. With his hands lower, he won't get as much leverage into his swing. Instead, he'll need to rely more on fast, strong leg and hip action to generate power and clubhead speed, as both Trevino and Palmer do so well. But if you find a golfer who gets both leverage, from an upright swing, *and* strong leg action, then you have an exceptionally long hitter

—like Nicklaus. For this reason I think the general trend among the pros is towards combining powerful, fast leg action with relatively upright swing plane.

Now that we know where the club should lie at the top of the swing, we can complete the picture of the shape of the swing from this viewing angle. I'd like you to do this by visualizing that the clubhead moves along the same path during the downswing as it did during the backswing. (This is how it should appear when you are looking down the target line *(Illustration 18)*. Later, when you view the swing from a different angle, we'll see that the two paths are not exactly the same.)

Again, we're talking about a simple swing — the ideal swing, I feel. You can find any number of fine players who "drop" the club into a lower path — a flatter plane than they had going back — as they move into their downswing. A very few — Bobby Jones was one — even loop it the other way. They return the clubhead along a more upright plane. But despite the number of fine players who switch to a different track for the downswing, I still feel that there are fewer moving parts — and thus less chance of error — if the clubhead moves back and forward, up and down, on more or less the same plane.

At this point I'd like to make a final review of how the swing should look when viewed down the shot line. The clubhead starts back along the line for several inches before moving inside. Then it continues back and up until the club lays about parallel with the target line — forming the left "rail."

On the downswing the clubhead appears — from this angle — to move along the same path. It moves from inside to along the target line. Finally it returns to inside the line as it continues up and around on the follow-through.

Now let's look at the shape of the swing from

Play with a simple swing

(Illustration 18) While successful golfers have played with swing planes that vary between backswing and downswing (smaller drawings), such variation adds complexity to the stroke. Ideally, you should imagine your swing as going back and up and down and forward on the same plane. This simpler swing minimizes the chance for error.

a different angle — "face-on." Assume that you-the-viewer are facing you-the-golfer.

When we watched ourselves swing from the previous angle, we realized that the clubhead had to be moving along the target line during impact to hit the ball straight. From this new angle, if we could run our swings in slow motion, we'd soon discover equally important principles about striking a golf ball.

First, we'd see that the ball will not fly straight unless the clubface is looking down the target line during impact. The leading edge of the clubface must form a 90-degree, or "square," angle with the target line as the ball is struck. The ball will not fly straight if the clubface looks either left or right of the line.

The second thing we'd see is that the clubface must be traveling at ball level during impact. It might be descending slightly, but it must make contact at ball level. Solid contact is impossible when the center of the face strikes under the ball, or above its back-center. If the face hits below the ball, "fat" or scuffed shots result. On topped shots the clubface will be largely above the ball's equator.

Imagine that the clubhead is a ball at the end of a chain that swings back and forth. From our present vantage point we see that this swinging ball moves downward and forward toward the golf ball. It reaches the lowest point of its arc at the golf ball and then moves upward gradually as it continues forward.

If this swinging ball were the clubhead, its equator would be at exact ball level only when the clubhead reached the lowest point of its arc, at that split-second in time and space when it wasn't moving either downward or upward. Ideally, it is at this point in the swing that the clubface should meet the ball.

What happens if the clubhead doesn't reach the ball until it's already started moving upward? Usually you will "top" the shot. There is very little leeway to impact the ball after your club has reached the lowest part of its arc. This works only when the ball is sitting up on a tee or high on some grass.

Fortunately, club manufacturers have given us a little leeway in the other direction. They have built enough loft into clubs so that it is possible to strike the ball just a shade *before* the clubhead reaches its lowest point, yet still make solid contact and get the shot airborne.

This built-in leeway increases with the loft of the club. If you are swinging a 2-iron with its fairly small amount of loft, you'd better meet the ball very near the bottom of the arc, almost precisely when the center of the clubface is at the equator of the ball. If the clubhead is still descending when you reach the ball with this iron, you'll hit an extremely low shot. With the highly-lofted 9-iron, however, you can contact the ball well before reaching the bottom of your arc and still get decent height on the shot.

However, I suggest that you do *not* think in terms of striking down on the ball with the more-lofted clubs and sweeping away your shots with longer, less-lofted irons and woods. Why make a conscious effort to alter your swing from shot to shot? Why complicate the game unnecessarily? Merely play the ball farther forward — say opposite the left heel — on those long shots that you want to sweep away. Then play it an inch or two farther back toward stance-center on the shorter irons. By slightly altering the ball's position this way, you can make more or less the same swing with each club (although actually the different lengths of your clubs will automatically produce some variety in the shape of your swing.)

From what I've said here you might assume that the bottom of the clubhead's path as seen from this angle is identical to that of the ball swinging on the end of the chain. This isn't quite so, and it isn't the image that you should have of the shape of the swing, except, as we noted, on putts. The modern player does certain things in his swing that extend the length of the clubhead's movement at ball level before it begins to move upward. For one thing, by maintaining a slight flex in his left knee *through* impact he avoids stiffen-

ing and raising his left side. He "stays down[ ]
the shot — and so does his clubhead.

Thus the path of the clubhead through the ball,
as you should imagine it, is more level just after
impact than just before impact. Imagine that the
clubhead is an airplane coming down for a landing. It gradually flies lower until it reaches the
runway — ball level. Then it rolls forward along
the runway — at ball level.

The path of the clubhead going back, away from
the ball during the takeaway, takes on just the
opposite pattern. At this stage, you want to establish width in your swing. You want a nice, full
extension of your left arm. The clubhead should
move back fairly level and low to the ground for
a few inches. Imagine an airplane taking off in the
opposite direction, rolling down the runway and
then gradually swinging into the air *(Illust. 19)*.

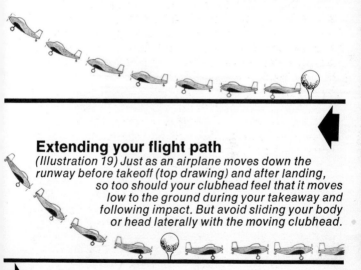

Extending your flight path

*(Illustration 19) Just as an airplane moves down the
runway before takeoff (top drawing) and after landing,
so too should your clubhead feel that it moves
low to the ground during your takeaway and
following impact. But avoid sliding your body
or head laterally with the moving clubhead.*

...er in visualizing such clubhead paths ...from and back to the ball is that you ...mpted to level out your clubhead path ...your body laterally in the direction the ...ving. While it's fine to imagine the clubhead going back low and swinging through low, it's also necessary to imagine your head as the "hub" of your swing. Always keep it centered in its original place and you will not sway.

Now let's start to fill in the picture of the clubhead's path. It moves back and over the shoulders. But then, from your present vantage point, you'll see that it descends to the ball a bit more steeply than it ascended going back *(Illustrations 20a and 20b).* It moves down along a line that is slightly

Shape of backswing (side view)
(Illustration 20a) The clubhead moves away from the ball low to the ground and into a wide semi-circle. This width is established by the extension of the left arm, which forms a straight-line continuation of the clubshaft until the wrists' hinging becomes evident. Ideally, your clubshaft should not swing past horizontal at the top of the swing.

closer to the golfer. This change in path occurs because, during his downswing, the player shifts his legs and hips farther to his left than they were during the backswing. This shift to the left also forces his wrists to stay hinged and his right arm to remain bent at the elbow, thus bringing the clubhead in closer to his body than it had been going back. Only after impact, as his right arm reaches full extension, does his swing take on the width that it had during his backswing.

Thus we've seen that the clubhead should start back low and level from the ball, and move back and up in a wide part-circle. Then it should return down and forward on a sharper angle of descent,

Shape of downswing (side view)
(Illustration 20b) Though your head should not shift toward the target during the downswing, your knees should slide in that direction at the very start. The left knee leads everything else into the ball. This shift to the left brings the clubhead back to the ball on a path that is inside of that it described during the backswing. Your clubhead should be either at ball level, or still descending slightly, during impact.

yet extend low and level once again through impact before continuing upward in a wide part-circle *(Illustration 19).*

All that now remains to complete our picture of the shape of the swing from this angle is the length of the backswing. For years many teachers and players felt that you should swing back *at least* far enough to put your clubshaft in a horizontal position. Thankfully, this misconception is rapidly disappearing, largely because so few of today's top players on the pro tour reach horizontal, even on their drives.

The swing has become shorter over the years as we've realized that the length of one's swing — beyond a certain point — has nothing to do with adding length to the shot. The purposes of the backswing are merely to build up maximum potential energy, and to put the club into a position from where it can be returned squarely to the ball in a way that releases this energy during impact.

For the vast majority of golfers, the club need not go beyond horizontal in order to build maximum potential energy. Once you've created this kinetic energy by turning your shoulders as far as you can, why go farther? Why add to the complexity of your swing by flipping your hands and wrists all over the place in an effort to extend its length? Why sacrifice control? In visualizing the shape of your backswing, I suggest you imagine that the club moves no farther back than to horizontal, if that far, on drives.

Now that we've seen the shape of the efficient golf swing, I'll again caution you not to try to alter your swing to make it conform. You'll be better off if you don't clutter your mind with "key moves" and "vital positions."

Instead, I'm now going to describe how you should set up to the ball so that you'll have a chance to make a swing that has a good shape to it. I'd like you to see if your set-up technique —

your stance, posture and alignment — meets my standards, and to alter it if it doesn't. Only after you have a good set-up to the ball will you be able to automatically and subconsciously produce the proper shape of swing when I tell you how it should feel.

The first thing that determines whether or not you have a good address position is simply how you position your clubhead behind the ball — how you aim the clubface. Time and again I see pupils — even low-handicap players — who mis-aim the clubface. A player will aim, let's say, out to the right of the target. He'll think his clubface is square to the target line. He'll even swear to it. Then I'll lay a club down on the ground, extending it out from his clubface along what he thinks is the target line. I'll say, "Is this club laying along the target line?" He'll say, "Yes, it is." Then I'll ask him to step back and check it. He'll then see how far off to the right of the real target he'd been aiming. He'll see how badly he's mis-aligned his clubface. And, chances are good that if he's mis-aligning with one club, he's mis-aligning with all clubs, including the putter.

If a player mis-aligns his clubface, if he's aiming down the wrong target line, he'll automatically adjust his feet and his body to this wrong line. He'll then swing the clubhead along this incorrect flight path. If he succeeds, he'll never hit a straight shot. He'll be forced to move his clubhead across, rather than along, the correct target line during impact. As we've seen, this is not the shape of swing you need to hit straight shots.

To hit straight shots consistently, you must first assume a correct grip (as described in Chapter 2), look down the target line from behind the ball, visualize the flight of a straight shot down the line, and then place your clubhead behind the ball so that it faces down that line.

Have a friend check your alignment of the club

periodically. Most of the top pros do this whenever their shots start flying off line. Assuring yourself of proper clubface alignment is the first step to take in bringing your shots back on target.

If you find that you are mis-aligning your clubface, you must force yourself to accept your mistake and go about correcting your aim. At times you won't believe that the correct alignment is really correct. If you've become accustomed to aiming, say, to the right, and then you start aiming correctly, you'll swear you're going to hit the ball to the left. Never mind. *Make* yourself aim the clubhead and swing along this seemingly incorrect line. Soon it will seem normal.

I've found it helps my pupils aim properly if they pay attention to the two vertical lines on the faces of most iron clubs, or the vertical edges of the inserts in the faces of their woods. I tell them to extend these vertical lines and visualize them as forming a "one-lane highway" to the target. I only wish that manufacturers would put a third line running between the two vertical lines on the faces, and then extend it across the top of clubs — as they often do across the tops of putters. This line would "divide" our "highway" and really give players a direct visual guide for proper aiming.

I think one reason why so many people have so much trouble seeing the proper target line, once they are over the ball, is because they tilt their own head incorrectly. The way you position your head determines the way you look at the ball. And the way you look at the ball obviously determines what target line — correct or incorrect — you see.

Ideally, an imaginary line across your eyes as you address the ball should be parallel with the *correct* target line. Let's say you position your head so that your eye-line extends to the right of target. You'll assume that what you see is the correct target line. You'll aim the clubface and you'll try to swing the clubhead through the ball along it.

To visualize the proper target line, your eye-line must be parallel to that correct line. It's relatively easy for golfers to assume the proper eye-line if they are playing the ball directly opposite their nose. All they have to do is look straight out into the distance with their eyes level, and then lower their vision to the ball.

In most instances, however, we play the ball out to the left of our nose, more opposite our left heel. To view the ball in this forward position, the tendency is to tilt the head slightly clockwise, thus raising the left eye and lowering the right. In so doing, our eye-line swings around so that it now extends to the right of target. This immediately gives us an incorrect impression of the target line. What appears to be the correct line to the target actually extends to the right of target, parallel to our eye-line. But since our eyes tell us this is the correct line, we aim the clubface down this line and align our stance, hips and shoulders — and our clubface — with it, to the right of target.

After flying a few shots to the right of target, the tendency is for us to start making compensations in our swing. The normal reaction to keep shots from flying right is to swing the clubhead more to the left. Then the clubhead must move on an outside-to-inside-the-line path. It cuts across the ball and applies the slice spin that's so familiar to so many golfers.

When we see our shots slicing to the right, we unconsciously begin aligning ourselves more and more to the left. This merely accentuates the outside-in path of the clubhead through the ball, adding more and more slice spin.

The only way to break the pattern is to start over and find the *correct* target line. Then aim down it — keeping our eye-line parallel to it — and swing the clubhead along it.

I've found that many of our great players — Nicklaus is one example — set the clubface squarely behind the ball, looking down the correct target line. Next they position their feet and their body while keeping their eye-line parallel to this line. Then, just before they swing they turn their head slightly *counterclockwise* so that the right eye is a bit higher than the left. They make this slight head-cock without, however, altering their eye-line, which remains parallel to the correct target line.

Cocking the head in this direction makes it much easier to turn the shoulders fully and freely during your backswing. It makes it easier to work your left shoulder down and under. Then, if during your downswing your head begins to rotate clockwise, so that your left eye moves higher than the right, so much the better. This rotation clears the way for the right shoulder to swing down and *under* as it should during the downswing to make the clubhead swing back to the target line from inside, rather than outside, that line.

If I were you, I wouldn't spend a great deal of time trying consciously to rotate your head in this manner during the downswing and throughswing. It will happen naturally if you follow my advice in the next chapter.

But I do suggest that you be conscious of the importance of selecting the proper target line by setting up with the correct eye-line. Then tilt your head slightly counterclockwise — keeping your eye-line the same — to free up your backswing shoulder turn.

I think it's always good if pupils can relate their set-up position to the shape of the swing they hope to produce. I've stressed, for instance, that the clubhead must be moving along — not across —the target line during impact. Relating this fact to our address position, what's the best way to set-up to the ball to produce such a clubhead path?

Don't forget the eye-line

(Illustration 21) You will tend to swing your clubhead through the hitting area along the line that your eyes "tell" you is the target line. If your eyes tell you an incorrect target line, you will tend to swing the clubhead along the wrong line. You will not hit straight shots to the target. Try to first select the correct target line, and then set your eye-line parallel to it, just as you similarly align your feet, knees, hips and shoulders. If you rotate your head during your swing, or if you turn it slightly counterclockwise before starting your backswing, make sure that you turn it on the same plane as your over-all swing. Otherwise your eyes will tell you the wrong line.

First, you should align yourself parallel to the correct target line as you address the ball. Not only should your eye-line parallel the target line, but so should your toe-line, your hip-line and your shoulder-line — especially your shoulder-line *(Illustration 21)*. The angle of your shoulder-line during impact directly determines the path your clubhead will be moving along when it strikes the ball. If your shoulder-line points to the right or left of target at impact, your clubhead will be moving in that direction — across, rather than along, the target line.

So make sure that your shoulders parallel the target line at address. Having your hip-line and toe-line parallel to the target line will help assure proper shoulder alignment. Each connects to the other. Each affects the other.

The best way I know to square yourself parallel to the target line is first to visualize that line, from the ball to the target. Then cross that line at 90-degrees with another imaginary line at the ball. This cross-line will extend to your left heel on full shots with woods and long irons. With the shorter clubs it will extend slightly closer to stance-center, but never more than two inches inside the left heel.

When you address the ball, merely make sure that your entire body is facing down this cross-line. If it does, then it has to be parallel to the target line.

A good practice drill that many pros use is to first lay a club down on the ground pointed toward a target. Cross this club with another at 90-degrees. Take a golf tee or your car key and make a slit in the grass alongside each club. Then lift the clubs and you can actually see the target line and the cross-line.

Practice shots with the ball placed at the center of the "X." Step out of position between shots to force yourself into the habit of setting-up parallel to the proper target line each time. Note where the ball seems to be positioned in relationship to your feet. Later, when you don't have your guide-lines, you'll want to recall this positioning. Do the same for the alignment of the clubface down the target line. Sense where it seems to be looking. You'll want to duplicate this sense of clubface alignment on the course.

Keep legs lively for longer shots

(Illustration 22) Imagine the lack of thrust a sprinter would experience if he started from a stiff-legged position. Stiff legs in golf, either at address or during the swing, similarly deprive you of power available in the big muscles of your calves and thighs.

The proper width for the stance varies with different players. Short stocky players, who use a lot of leg action as a source of power, generally assume wider stances than do tall, thin golfers who play the ball closer to their feet. These taller players rely more on leverage than leg action for power, and, thus, don't need such a wide stance. I suggest you place your heels more or less shoulder-width apart, depending on your individual physique.

You should point both feet straight forward at address, but after you've made your toe-line parallel to the target line, you should turn your left foot counterclockwise slightly. This may make your toe-line point slightly to the left of, instead of parallel to, the target line. But never mind. This slight toeing out will hardly be sufficient to alter your hip-line, let alone your shoulder-line. But it will make it easier for you to extend the path of your clubhead along the target line as it moves through the ball.

Your posture at address has as much to do with the shape of your swing as does the alignment of your feet, hips, shoulders and eye-line. If, for instance, your swing is to have proper shape, your left hand, arm and side must dominate. Your left arm must lead your right arm throughout your backswing, but if it sags at address, your right hand and arm may take over once the club is moving. So address the ball with your left shoulder high and your left arm extended. Your right shoulder will be slightly lower than your left, because your right hand is lower than your left on the club. Your right arm should feel passive, and it should be slightly folded in toward your side, bent at the elbow and ready to hinge during your backswing. Actually, it's a good idea to also have your right knee pointing slightly inward as well.

To assume a good posture over the ball, I suggest you first stand as erect as you can, like a West Point cadet at attention. You'll feel a little tension in back of your shoulders. Your back should feel nice and straight. Your chest should feel like it's sticking out, your stomach like it's pulling in.

Now ease your head *slowly* forward, bending only from your neck, until you are looking at the ball. As you lower your head, bend your knees *slightly.* Don't bounce on them. Just flex them enough to break any tension.

Finally, keeping your back straight, bring your hands forward and slide your right hand below your left into gripping position. Keep your left arm extended as I mentioned above. Fold your right elbow and knee in slightly.

That's it. Once you have this posture, and once you are aligned parallel to the target line, then you're ready to make a simple, efficient swing of proper shape.

Now it's time to learn just how this swing should feel.

CHAPTER SIX
HOW YOUR SWING SHOULD FEEL

I'd like you to imagine that you are sitting in a canoe in the middle of a small lake *(Illustration 23)*. Since one end of the lake is lower than the other, gravity pulls you in that direction, toward a small waterfall.

You sit in the canoe and you can feel it being pulled slowly toward the waterfall. It's a smooth pull—no jerks. But as you get closer, the pull gradually becomes stronger and stronger. The boat moves faster and faster. You can't stop it. Suddenly you're over the waterfall, swoosh . . . splash . . . and you're hurtling down the stream.

This is just one of many images I use to relate the feel of the proper downswing to my pupils. Your clubhead is just like that canoe. It starts from an almost static position. Then it begins to move slowly, then gradually faster, but always smoothly. It's being pulled down and forward toward the ball, faster, faster, and then, "pow," and it's gone, lashing through the ball and beyond.

Many pupils react favorably to this analogy. They begin to start their downswing slowly and smoothly instead of with one big jerk. They begin *swinging* the clubhead instead of pushing and shoving it. They start whipping the clubhead *through* the ball and beyond, rather than merely swinging *at* it.

Timing your downswing

(Illustration 23) The feel of the proper downswing is similar to that you would experience if you were sitting in a canoe being gradually drawn toward a waterfall. You should feel that your legs and left arm are pulling the clubhead toward the ball, slowly at first, then faster and faster until it "swooshes" through. This feeling of gradual acceleration will occur only if your shoulders follow, rather than lead, your legs.

In this chapter I'm going to present you with a wide variety of mental pictures similar to that of the canoe in the lake. I'm going to tell you how your swing should feel.

Already you've developed a feel for the "part-swing" shots—putts, chips and pitch shots. You've found your basic swing rhythm by experimenting

with full shots with your most-lofted club. You've felt solid contact with the ball and seen your shots succeed. You've experienced sensations of good swing motion and smooth acceleration. You've built yourself some success patterns. Finally, you know how the full swing should look—its shape.

With this background, along with the sensations of feel I'll give you now, you will be able, with practice, to produce a much-improved, if not outstanding, golf swing. Read this chapter carefully and give it a good deal of thought. Then take your most-lofted club and go out and hit full shots, *always within your basic rhythm,* until you feel yourself making a successful swing. Gradually work back to the less-lofted clubs. If you falter along the way, return to a more-lofted club, or even your part-swing shots, until you re-establish your success pattern, until you regain the feel of a proper swing on these simpler shots.

Many of the sensations I'll describe or observations I'll make in this chapter may not register with you. Don't worry, this is normal. Every competent teacher of golf knows that he or she must find many different ways to explain the same point. Every pupil has had a different background, different experiences in life. We can't expect everyone to be able to relate to the same explanations. If you've never been out in a canoe, you may not be able to relate to the example of the canoe in the lake. But if I described the same feeling for the downswing in other terms—perhaps that it's like a piece of paper or wood rushing along a rain-filled gutter towards a city drain—you might get the picture.

Please don't assume that, by trying to duplicate the sensations of feel that I describe, you'll be mimicking Bob Toski's swing. As a tournament player, even before I began teaching golf, I made it a practice to question other pros on how various facets of the swing felt to them. Later, on the lesson tee, I've benefited from the feedback my pupils give me as to how incorrect and correct swing movements feel to them. In short, I'm not going to tell you how *my* swing feels. I'm going to tell you how *your* swing should feel.

After you read and understand *mentally* how the swing should feel, you must work toward developing a given *physical* sensation. I'll tell you, for instance, the proper sequence of movement you should employ during your downswing. Then I'll tell you how it feels to make this sequence of movement. It will be up to you to practice until it feels right in your swing. *BUT NEVER TRY TO ACHIEVE MORE THAN ONE SENSATION IN EACH SWING.*

You'll know when you've found the right feeling. You may say, "That feels entirely different from what I've been doing. No wonder I couldn't do it right. I understood what to do, but I couldn't feel it." You'll not only react consciously to the correct feeling, but subconsciously you'll store it away in the "computer" of your mind. Then you should continue to strengthen this feeling through practice.

Finally, on the course during play, you'll merely summon forth whatever feeling you need to duplicate whatever shot you've visualized beforehand. You will be playing golf by feel.

OVERALL SWING SENSATIONS

Nobody ever hit the ball on their backswing. Yet, many golfers take the club back so fast that it seems like they're trying to do just that. It's no wonder they lose control of the club. Then, on the downswing, they lose a great deal of clubhead speed simply because they must burn up so much energy trying to regain club control.

Others swing back too methodically, then slash at the ball with their arms because they feel they must do something to make the club move faster. They never get much clubhead speed because they don't use their legs. Whatever speed they do generate is wasted before impact because they use their hands too soon.

A good mental image for these golfers is that of an automobile stuck in mud or snow. Recall how you'd try to "rock" the car out. You would put it in "reverse" and slowly roll the wheels up the back edge of the rut. Then you'd put it in forward gear and slowly—to avoid spinning the wheels—accelerate. You'd keep doing this, slowly taking the car back and up until it's in position to gradually accelerate forward. Back slow, then gradually faster forward. Picture this in your mind. Sense how it would feel inside the car. Imagine the same movement back and forward when you swing the golf club.

Or think of yourself as a rubber band. A rubber band is like your muscles. It can stretch and contract.

If you stretch the rubber band too far, it will break. It loses its tension. If you stretch your muscles too far during your backswing, something will collapse to relax the tension. You may loosen your grip; or your left arm may bend; or your left wrist may bow inward; or your body may sway. Something has to give sooner or later.

If you stretch a rubber band fully, and then let go, you get a powerful "snap" *(Illustration 24)*. This is what happens during your downswing if you retain your left side's stretching, if you keep your left arm extended, and if your right arm and wrist stay bent or cocked until near impact.

But if you stretch a rubber band between your hands and then move your hands back together, relaxing the tension, it won't snap. That's what happens when your right shoulder and right hand take over on your downswing. You release your stretch too soon, before impact. No snap.

Around Old Baldy Lodge in Wyoming where I used to teach in the summer, you can see a lot of deer. The graceful springing action they make—the agility, the speed, the distance they can jump—is really fantastic. Yet these supple animals do not have big muscles and tendons and bones in their legs. What they do have is great flexibility and smoothness of movement—springlike action.

You don't see the deer stand rigid and stiff be-

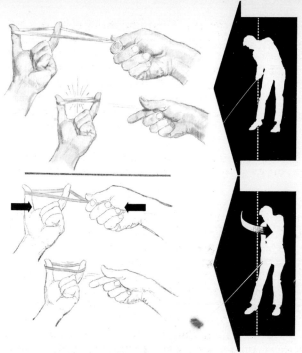

Delay your release of energy

(Illustration 24) Most golfers tend to dissipate much of their potential energy before the clubhead reaches the ball. If your knees slide to the left at the start of the downswing, while your head and shoulders stay "back," you will achieve the same dynamic transfer of energy to the ball that you feel when releasing a fully-stretched rubber band. If, however, your shoulders race ahead of your legs and lower body during the down-swing, the effect will be the same as if the fully-stretched rubber band had been partially relaxed before it was released.

fore they jump. They'd lose their agility. They'd get tense, and tension and stiffness inhibit movement in everything, including the golf swing. Perhaps you stand over the ball too long before you start your swing.

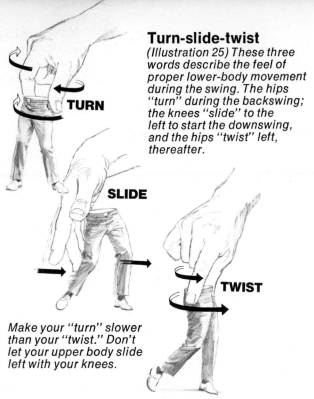

Turn-slide-twist

(Illustration 25) These three words describe the feel of proper lower-body movement during the swing. The hips "turn" during the backswing; the knees "slide" to the left to start the downswing, and the hips "twist" left, thereafter.

TURN

SLIDE

TWIST

Make your "turn" slower than your "twist." Don't let your upper body slide left with your knees.

As far as your lower body is concerned, the golf swing is nothing more than a *turn,* a *slide,* and a *twist.* You *turn* on the backswing, *slide* toward the target as you start your downswing, then *twist* to your left just before your hands lead the clubhead into the ball *(Illustration 25). Turn, slide, twist.* These are the key words you should learn to feel. *Turn, slide, twist.* Actually, the twist is like the turn, but faster.

Many golfers turn going back and twist coming through, but they leave out the slide. To slide, you must feel you are starting your downswing with your lower body and legs moving laterally to the left. If your right shoulder or right hand take over at the start down, you can't slide. You'll just twist.

Other golfers turn and slide, but forget to twist. They "block out" with their left hip. These golfers should learn to feel that they are starting their downswing with their knees flexed and sliding, but with their hips turning.

And make your movements smooth, like the canoe floating on the lake. It's "turn," "slide," "twist"—not "lift," "shove," "jerk."

The place where you can really feel the motion of your golf swing is in the movement of your arms. Try swinging a golf club with your eyes closed. Without the ball in view to distract you, and with your sense of sight eliminated temporarily, you become acutely aware of the motion of your arms as they move back and forward. You'll feel the rhythm of your swing.

How should this motion of the arms feel in the proper golf swing? It should feel the same as if you were walking briskly down the street and your arms were swinging back and forth in normal fashion. You'll be swinging your arms in a different direction and on a different plane, but the *feeling of motion* should be the same. If you take your sense of arm motion while walking and apply it to your sense of arm motion while swinging a golf club, you'll generate more clubhead speed than you ever dreamed possible.

But it's not easy to swing a golf club with the same freedom of arm movement that you have when walking. Most golfers display this kind of freedom when they take a practice swing. But then, with the ball in front of them, and knowing that the next swing will count, they begin to over-control the club. Tension and stiffness set in. So does jerkiness. They lift the club going back, instead of swinging it with their arms. They shove the clubhead *at* the ball instead of swinging it *through* the ball and beyond.

If you can make a smooth arm motion during your practice swing, why not make it during your regular swing? You'll be surprised how much farther and straighter you'll hit the ball with much less effort.

Try this. Take a deep breath and then swing the club before you let out any air. I asked a friend of mine, Bill Michaels, to try this and he thought I was some kind of nut. But he soon found that it was all but impossible to tense up during his swing so long as he held his breath. It's a beautiful reaction. There is practically no way you can push or shove or force your swing. It's a great way to get the feeling of swinging your arms freely, without over-controlling the club.

Try it on your short-iron shots in practice. I'm not sure you can hold your breath long enough to make a full swing, but even if you exhale on your downswing, you'll still find it difficult to create much inner tension.

And try it on your putts. Feel your arms swinging back and through. You just might discover the freedom of clubhead movement you've been unable to muster under pressure.

If you are driving your car 20 miles an hour on a straight highway, you'll hold the steering wheel very lightly. Drive the same road at 70 miles per hour and you'll hold it more firmly. Then drive that same speed on a curving road and you'll hold on for dear life.

The golf swing also curves, and your clubhead accelerates from zero to 80-110 miles per hour. Obviously your hold on the club will change during your swing, just as it would on the steering wheel.

But this change in grip pressure should occur automatically—and smoothly. You should not even be aware that it's changing. When you practice you should try to *feel* that you are keeping the same grip pressure throughout your swing. Actually it will change, but smoothly, automatically. What we're trying to avoid is a sudden clenching of the club at some point, just as we try to avoid any sudden jerking or shoving. Clenching causes tension, and slows down your clubhead speed. Your arm motion should feel smooth and fluid throughout your downswing, and your grip pressure should *feel* constant, even though it really isn't.

Your hold on the club should feel consistently *light*—not loose or tight—throughout your swing. Also, the pressure of *one hand against the other* should remain constant.

As you swing, imagine that your hands are like a good dance team. They're close against each other, moving together. There's never any separation between the two. The man—your left hand— is the leader. Your right hand responds to your left, but they never move apart or squeeze together tightly *(Illustration 26).*

Watch different pros playing in a tournament, live or on TV, and you'll soon find one whose swing gives off to you a sense of rhythm that you feel you can adapt to your own game. Visualize the pace of that player's swing over and over in your mind's eye. Then try to duplicate it in your practice sessions.

I've always loved to watch Sam Snead's swing. I've tried to emulate the sense of rhythm that it conveys. He never seems to be in a hurry to place the club in position at the top of his swing. He's never in any rush to swing it back to the ball.

I don't think there is a simpler or better way to get the feel of smooth rhythm and proper timing than through practicing your putting. It's a shame that so many golfers find putting practice so boring; they'd rather go out and slug away with a driver.

Whenever your timing feels haywire, practice putting for a while. Then move on to chipping, pitching and, gradually, full shots. Merely concentrate on making solid contact with the ball. This

Hands feel unified
(Illustration 26) Imagine that your hands blend together throughout your swing like a good dance team. The left hand controls the right, gently and smoothly, just as the male dancer leads the female. The two partners never separate.

will force you to eventually start making well-timed strokes. And this new-found sense of timing and smooth rhythm will carry over into your longer shots.

It's important to hit some full shots before every round to loosen your muscles. But it's also important to stroke a few putts to re-establish your basic swing rhythm.

You'll know when you've made a good swing. It will feel ridiculously effortless. You'll feel like you could have hit the ball 10-20 yards farther.

ADDRESS POSITION SENSATIONS

The club will actually feel thinner some days than others. It's best when it does. And it will feel thin more often if you hold it lightly with just enough pressure to control its movement—no more, no less.

As you address the ball, don't squeeze any part of either hand, but *feel* or *sense* that you are going to control the club with the last three fingers of your left hand. These three fingers should feel ready to "rule" both hands throughout your swing. Your right hand should feel as if it's doing little more than caressing the club.

Your knees should feel positioned so that if you bounced on them they'd bend toward the ball. To get this feeling, you must point your right knee slightly inward to the left. Your left side should feel slightly stretched as a result, even though your left knee is also flexed slightly. What you're doing is more or less previewing your impact position at address. Why not?

Even though your right knee is bent inward slightly, you should still feel that most of your weight is on your left foot, especially on short iron shots. With your weight slightly to the left at address, you'll find it easier to let your left side control your backswing, as it should.

You should feel as if you're standing on the ball and heel of each foot, but not on the toes.

BACKSWING SENSATIONS

Your hands should feel "quiet" during the start of your backswing, as if they weren't even there. You should feel motion in your arms, but not in your hands.

Lay your left palm face down on the top of a table. Now, bend your wrist *without lifting your palm from the table.* Bend it so that you see wrinkles at the base of your thumb. This is the only movement of this hand and wrist that you should feel throughout your backswing, and then only near the top of your swing, as a reaction to the weight of the moving club *(Illustration 27).*

Too often a player spoils his swing by increasing his grip pressure while he addresses the ball and during his takeaway. If you had sufficient control of the club before you put it down behind the ball, there is no reason to increase this control to any substantial degree while you are setting up to the ball and swinging the clubhead away. Increasing your grip pressure at this point merely tightens your arm and shoulder muscles, and thus restricts your backswing.

Try addressing the ball with the clubhead off the ground. Swing it back from this mid-air position. You may not hit the shot squarely, but you'll get the feel for proper control—rather than over-control—of the club.

During your backswing your arms should feel as if they are moving as a result of your shoulders turning. You should not feel any "wrist action." Never feel that you are lifting the club with your hands and arms. *Imagine* that the clubhead is attached to your left shoulder and that it won't swing back and up unless your shoulder swings around and under your chin.

Your right arm and right side should feel as if they are asleep during your backswing. Your left hand, arm and shoulder should be able to move them aside at will. The feeling of a passive right side is vital, since this side tends to enforce its natural dominance as soon as the club leaves the ground. If this happens, your right elbow will move too far out from your side and your right shoulder muscles will tighten. Both of these results will block your shoulder turn. You'll merely pick the club up with your hands and arms. You won't get the power build-up you need to generate maximum force into the ball.

There's no big secret about making a full shoul-

Ideal wrist action during backswing

(Illustration 27) Many golfers become too floppy-wristed at the top of the backswing, and thus lose control of the club. Ideally, the only left-hand wrist action that most golfers need to feel during the backswing is a hinging at the base of the thumb. If you find wrinkles occurring at the back of this wrist, instead of below the thumb, you should seek more left-hand firmness during your backswing, especially in the last three fingers. Improper hinging also occurs if backswing is too fast or too long.

der-turn during the backswing. All you must do is simply turn your right shoulder "out of the way."

Try standing erect facing straight out. Then imagine that someone behind you has called your name. Without shifting the position of your feet, turn around to see who's calling. I'll bet that you turn your shoulders *at least* a full 90 degrees.

Some people can make a bigger shoulder turn than others. So what? What really matters is not how *far* you can turn, but that you turn as *far as you can*. On the course, your turn should not require any conscious effort.

If you are a more-advanced player with a long

backswing, you will get a much more effective wind-up if you "resist" with your legs while turning your shoulders. Keep your right knee flexed throughout your backswing. Never feel that you've let your weight shift to the outside of your right foot.

During your backswing imagine that you're standing on a slick floor, or even a sheet of ice, without any spikes on your shoes. This will force you to "hold on" with your feet. It will give you the proper leg resistance you should feel during your backswing.

The speed of your backswing largely determines how well you control the club. If you swing your arms back too fast, you'll force yourself to clench harder with your hands. This will cause tension and restrict a full, free shoulder turn. You should swing back just fast enough to establish a sense of rhythm.

If you've played a racquet sport such as tennis, you know that as you prepare to return the shot you're not even aware of making a backstroke. The ball, because it's moving, occupies your full attention. You don't have time to think about *how* you are moving the racquet back. Consequently, a good tennis player will unconsciously swing his racquet back and turn his shoulders without any rush or hurry. It's a smooth turning away.

In golf the ball is stationary. We have plenty of time to dwell on how we're going to make our backswing. This awareness often creates anxiety that causes us to rush to the top of our swing.

Try to feel that your golfing backswing has the same pace that you'd give your tennis backstroke. Remember that in golf, as in tennis, all you are really doing on your backswing is placing yourself and your club in position to drive the ball forward.

TOP-OF-SWING SENSATIONS
You should feel a slight tension, just a little dis-

comfort, across your back and down your l___
at the top of your backswing. This indicates
you've built up some kinetic energy to be releas__
later, during impact.

If you don't feel this slight discomfort, something has relaxed. You may have let your left arm
bend too much, or collapsed the back of your left
wrist into a "cuppy" concave position. You may
have swung your hands too far *around,* rather than
over, your back. Or you may simply have failed to
complete your turn.

Whatever caused you to relax has cost you distance—an "energy leak." You'll know you've completed your shoulder turn only when you feel this
slight discomfort. But if this discomfort becomes
so great that you're forced to relax something,
then you must reduce your turn.

The speed of your backswing, if too fast, can
cause your left arm, or your wrists, to collapse at
the top of your swing. Think of your left arm as a
cable with an object—the club—on the end. If you
swing back too fast, the weight of the object moving over and past your back will bend the cable.
If you swing back too slow, the outward pulling—
centrifugal force—of the object won't be strong
enough to keep the cable straight. You must keep
your cable extended to avoid any "energy leak."
But remember that your left arm is a "cable"—not
a steel pipe or a rubber hose.

I understand it's a principle of physics that a
moving object tends to keep moving until it en-
counters some resistance. Near the top of your
backswing, therefore, your moving clubhead will
want to keep moving over your shoulders. The
downward pull of gravity also encourages it to
keep extending its arc. You should feel resistance
to this movement in the last three fingers of your
left hand, since these fingers are farthest from the
moving clubhead.

If you are controlling the club at the top of your

with these three fingers, you may
increase in their gripping pressure.
ngers in control you'll be in good
the club back to the ball with your
rm and hand leading the way.

Unfortunately, most right-handed people follow
the natural pattern of letting their right hand resist
the moving clubhead and thus take over control of
the club at the top of the backswing. This opens
the door for a right-hand dominant throwing action on the downswing, resulting in premature releasing of energy and flipping of the clubhead
across, rather than along, the target line.

Should you pause at the top of your swing? I'm
told that the club never really stops moving, but I
do think that many golfers experience the *feeling*
of a very slight pause. I don't think this is a good
feeling to cultivate if it feels unnatural and offends
your basic sense of rhythm. But I do think it's a
good feeling to strive for if you often swing too
fast—if you tend to move into your downswing before you've completed your backswing. The feeling of pausing will give you a greater sensation
that you are in control of the club as it changes
direction.

Your hands should feel "quiet," but firm, at the
top of your swing. You should feel as if you've
"placed" the club into position, and that your left
hand is ready to pull it back to the ball.

Swing your club to the top of your backswing
and then stop. Where on your feet do you feel your
weight? Ideally it should seem more or less equally
distributed between the inner half of your right
foot and the inner half of your left foot. Your weight
on your right foot should feel more toward the
heel, on your left foot more toward the sole.

DOWNSWING SENSATIONS

We've seen that the backswing is a "package
deal" with everything moving together as a one-

piece unit, nothing moving faster than anything else.

The downswing of a good golfer may also look unified to some people, but we've learned from high-speed movies and photos that it really isn't. The downswing is really a sequence of movements. If everything moves in proper sequence, we have proper "timing." The clubhead will move *along* the target line through the ball, and it will do so without having lost any of its speed before impact. When our timing is off, when we move out of proper sequence, we usually throw the clubhead *across* the line. And we usually "release" our stored-up potential energy before impact.

The overall feeling you should have on your downswing is that, first, your left heel is returning to the ground and pulling your knees and hips laterally to the left. These, in turn, are pulling your left arm down and forward and your right elbow into your side. Your arms are leading your hands and your clubhead is lagging behind everything. Then, suddenly, you experience the *reaction* of the wrists unhinging and the clubhead squaring up to, and lashing through, the ball. If your timing is correct, this uncocking of the wrists will feel automatic, with no conscious effort on your part.

All the parts of this downswing sequence follow each other so closely that it's difficult to discern that, say, your legs are moving before your arms. But you should definitely feel that your feet and legs are moving ahead of your shoulders.

One of the surest ways to ruin your timing is to race your shoulders into your downswing. This is especially a problem for golfers who don't complete their shoulder turn on their backswing. When your shoulders move too soon on your downswing, you throw your clubhead out of its proper path. It cuts across the target line instead of swinging along the line and "through" the ball. Your shoulders are "followers," not leaders, in the proper downswing.

The problem is that most of us relate power to our back and shoulders instead of our legs. Naturally, whenever we try to hit the ball far, we rely too heavily—and too early—on our shoulders. This destroys the proper sequence of movement—timing.

The golfer who starts learning on the putting green, and then moves back to chip and pitch shots before attempting full swings, is less likely than most to suffer from "racing shoulders." Since these part-swing shots don't require much shoulder turn, they give him a chance to develop the feel of arm motion, which is the essence of swing rhythm.

If your shoulders come into play too soon in your downswing—you are probably slicing or pulling your shots—I suggest you practice part-swing shots of 40-60 yards. Try to feel that on your downswing you are swinging with your arms and legs, but holding back the return movement of your shoulders.

A good feeling to have is that your downswing takes less effort than did your backswing. You should feel that your club is lagging and that you are *hoping* it catches up. Never feel that you are *forcing* it to catch up.

You should feel that your right hand is responding to your left hand, not vice-versa, in your downswing, just as it did going back. Your right hand is just going along for the ride. After the ball is away, you may feel as if you hit it with your right hand, but this is a *reaction.* Most golfers should never actually try to throw their right hand into the shot.

The great striker of the ball is the golfer who can accelerate his hands through the hitting area without letting his right hand take over his left and force the back of his left wrist to bend inward. If you look at pictures of Jack Nicklaus swinging, you'll see that his left wrist is still firm and straight at the finish of his swing. It's still in control.

Imagine that you are holding a golf ball very lightly in your fingers and tossing it toward a wall with an easy underhand-sidearm motion. This is the relaxed flowing motion you should feel with your right arm and hand as you swing down and through the ball.

Imagine that you are holding a rug-beater in your left hand. You've got a rug hanging on the line. You're standing toward one edge of the rug and you're going to *backhand* the swatter against the rug. Make this motion, never letting the back of your left wrist collapse. You hit and hold. This is the firmness your left hand should feel as it moves into and through the hitting area *(Illustration 28)*.

To put these two feelings together, take a 7-iron and hit some shots in this fashion. Swing the club down and into the ball as you normally do, but then "hold" firm with your left wrist and arm immediately after impact. Try to finish your swing as soon as possible after you've struck the ball. Hit and hold.

This drill will give you the proper feeling of hand movement through impact. You'll feel as if they are moving under control, but with authority. You'll feel a bit of a snap that you won't experience when you try to overpower the ball with your right shoulder.

You'll also be building up the left-hand control that most golfers lack. You'll probably be surprised how far you follow-through before you can stop the club's forward movement.

Try slapping the open palm of your left hand with the open palm of your right hand. Hold your left hand still as if it were the golf ball at rest. Imagine that your right palm is the clubface. See what happens if you make contact with only the fingertips or the base of your right hand. This is comparable to the impact you get when you hit a

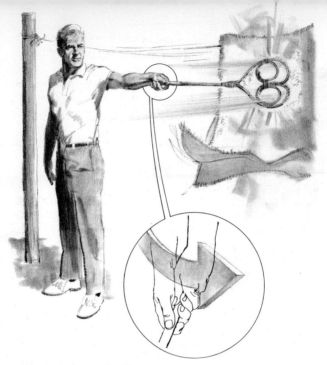

Left wrist feels firm

(Illustration 28) Your left wrist should feel as firm through impact as it would if you were backhanding with a rug-beater. You should feel no inward bending at either the top or back of your wrist.

golf ball with the toe or heel of the club.

Try pushing or shoving, rather than swinging, your right arm. Notice how much less snap, or "pop," you create. You get a dull thud because your muscles are tense. Keep slapping until you find the right hand-arm motion that gives you the most sting. That's approximately the same right-hand swinging motion you'll want to duplicate on your golf shots.

Terry Bradshaw, the great pro football quarterback, once told a friend of mine that when he passes a football he feels as if he's doing it with his forearm instead of his hand. It seems to him that his hand just happens to catch up and finally release the ball.

The downswing in golf is much the same. Obviously, we don't hit the ball with our forearms—we hit it with the clubhead—but the feeling should be that your forearms — not your hands — are swinging the club into position to hit the ball. Only at the last split-second should you feel your hands finally square the clubface and swing it through the ball.

As you move from part-swing to full-swing shots, the chances increase that your right hand will take over and break down your left wrist's dominance. When this happens, go back to your part-swing shots and stay with them until you re-establish left-hand control through impact. Through the ball, your left arm should feel that it is moving faster than your right.

Many golfers have trouble shifting onto their left side during their downswing. I think this stems from a fear that they won't get the ball into the air unless they stay back on their right foot and throw the clubface underneath it. Then what actually happens is that they throw the clubhead out beyond the target line early in the downswing, and thus cut across the line in the hitting area. Only by leading the downswing with your lower-left side —but with your head and shoulders staying "back" —will you swing the clubhead from inside to along the target line and into the ball.

If you hang a ball on a string from a tree limb so that it's about waist high and then ask a player to swing at it, he'll make a beautiful move onto his left foot. He does this easily because he senses that he'll have no trouble getting "under" the already-raised ball. A golfer will usually make this same smooth shift onto his left side if his ball is sitting on a tee. But if you lower the ball and set it on the grass, the same player often will stay back on his right foot during his downswing so he can slide the club under the ball.

One way to break this habit and help get your legs working correctly to your left at the start of your downswing is to tee the ball very high and a foot or so to the left of your left foot. Then actually step into the shot with your left foot, just as a baseball player steps into the pitch. You may miss the ball completely, but you'll get the feeling of leading to the left with your legs during your downswing.

Next, practice hitting shots without taking the step to the left, with the ball still teed high, but in normal position. Again, stress the feeling that your legs are pulling your arms, and finally the club, downward and forward.

Finally, gradually lower the tee more and more until you are playing the ball off the grass itself. But still keep the same feeling of pulling down and through with your left side, leveling the clubhead's path as it passes through the ball.

Can you visualize the pistons that drive the wheels on a steam engine? As they gradually move faster and faster, the wheels turn faster and faster and the engine moves faster and faster.

In golf your knees are the pistons. The faster they slide to the left at the start of your downswing, the faster everything else will follow, including the clubhead.

Just make sure that your knees don't jerk violently to the left. Like the pistons on the steam engine, they should move smoothly. If they don't your swing will "stutter."

If your left knee is pulling and leading properly, it should still feel flexed at impact. You should feel that it's moved farther to the left than any other part of your body, including your hips which have already started to twist.

At the top of your backswing, your left arm and your clubshaft will have formed an angle of more-or-less 90 degrees. If you start your downswing with your feet and legs pulling your arms down and forward to the left, you should feel that you are retaining this same angle until your hands are almost hip high.

It's natural that your grip pressure will increase during your downswing as your clubhead picks up speed. This happens without your thinking about it.

But golfers who hit *at* the ball, instead of *through* it, "over-grip." They grab with a tighter grip just before impact. This causes tension, and tension reduces clubhead speed. The ball doesn't go as far.

You really don't need very much grip pressure, even during impact. I prove this time and again to my pupils by making shots in which I actually *let go* of the club *before* impact. The club zings through the air down the fairway 40 or 50 yards, and the ball flies almost as far as on a normal shot. If it's possible to hit a shot almost normal distance without any hold on the club at impact, how much grip pressure do you really need on a regular shot?

When you swing *through* the ball and strike it squarely, it will feel "light" during impact. It will seem that it has jumped off the clubface quickly, as if it hadn't resisted the moving clubhead at all. The mis-hit shot will feel heavy and dull and slow in moving off the clubface. You will feel the ball's resistance.

The ball feels like a small marble when squarely struck. When you mis-hit, it feels more like you've struck the tee-marker.

You'll quickly learn the feeling of solid contact

if you start with putts and then work back to part-swing shots. Don't move on to longer shots until the ball feels light and quick coming off your putterface.

Anyone who has played much tennis knows the very different feel of a shot that rebounds off the center of the racquet from one that's struck out near the frame. There really is all the difference in the world in how the ball feels coming off the strings. You get a similar contrast in golf between the feel of an off-center strike and solid contact.

The serious tennis player will work for hours trying to achieve nothing more than the solid feel of solid central contact. Yet the golfer will think about everything else — his hands, his knees, his left thumb, right elbow, left arm and so on. He'd be better off, at least on the course, if he thought only about swinging the clubhead squarely through the ball, trying to capture the sensation of solid contact.

If you've timed your downswing properly, with your feet and legs leading your arms, and your hands and club lagging behind until impact, your clubhead will swing through the ball *along* the target line. You'll feel your hands continue out and up into a nice high position at the finish of your swing.

If you start your downswing with your right shoulder, you'll finish with your hands low and around your body. You'll feel as if you've swung at a baseball. You are forced into the low-finish position because your hands have swung the clubhead *across* the target line from outside to inside.

If you've made a well-timed downswing, not only will your hands finish high, but you'll feel your head has turned under, rotated clockwise with the turn of your shoulders. As your clubhead moves through the hitting area you should feel as though you are going to watch the flight of the ball by merely continuing this head rotation. You'll be looking "up" at the shot from "under" the ball, rather than "out" at the shot from "over" the ball.

As I mentioned earlier, the sensations I've described in this chapter are those that most golfers experience when they execute the swing properly. But not all golfers will be able to relate to all these sensations. Just pick those that make sense to you. And, above all, as you practice your full shots, never try to achieve more than one of these sensations during any given swing.

CHAPTER SEVEN
MAKE IT WORK ON THE COURSE

During practice a good basketball player may stand up to the free-throw line and make 10, 20 or even 30 shots in a row. Someone feeds him the ball after each shot and he just stands there and falls into a groove. His muscles respond almost automatically.

But then put the same player in a game situation, where he's moving around between free-throw attempts, where making these shots directly affects winning or losing, and he'll probably find it difficult to make even four or five free throws in a row.

It's exactly the same in golf, when you move from the practice field to the battlefield. Suddenly you find yourself having to count strokes. Because you're moving around between shots, your swing won't fall into a groove so readily. You're being watched and judged by other players. You're hitting from varying terrain instead of consistently level lies. Obviously, you are going to find it difficult, if not impossible, to duplicate the success you experienced during practice. Let's recognize that fact from the start, so that you won't become disappointed if you don't go out and shoot your "career round" the first time you try to play by feel on the course.

There are three ways to go about applying what

you've learned in practice to your actual play on the course:

First, you can go out to play with the optimistic attitude that you will employ, on the course, the new-found skills you've been practicing, and that you will succeed magnificently.

This is a very dangerous attitude. What usually happens is that your new method fails under the pressures and circumstances of actual play. Then you become disappointed, frustrated and, finally, doubtful of the new method itself. Chances are you will reject it. I've seen this happen time after time. The tendency for pupils to give themselves a lesson on the course is the biggest headache a teaching professional faces. And it's the biggest cause of anguish among pupils. You simply cannot work on a new swing technique on the course and still expect to shoot a good score.

The second approach is to realize the difficulty of shooting good scores immediately with a new swing. You make up your mind that you will stick with your new method during your round, but that you won't worry if it fails at first.

I've found that this approach isn't very realistic. Most golfers can't put up with failure during actual play, even if they expect it. Sooner or later they begin to question the new technique. Often they will reject it altogether.

The ideal approach to take when you go onto the course to play by feel for the first time is simply to forget about any specific swing instruction you've been practicing. Don't worry about any grip modifications. Don't fuss and fret about your posture over the ball. Don't think about any swing "tips," such as starting your downswing with your feet and legs, or holding back the unwinding of your shoulders.

Instead, merely visualize the shot you need and imagine how your swing should feel to make that shot. Then try to duplicate that feel both during your practice swing and your actual swing.

To master playing by feel you must overcome the normal habit of dwelling on swing specifics and replace it with the simple thought of merely hitting the ball to the target you've selected, along the trajectory you've visualized. You must learn to think about what your shot should look like and how your swing should feel, rather than what you should do in your swing.

If you do not concern yourself on the course with any specifics of grip, stance, posture and swing that you've been practicing, these changes will creep into your game automatically in varying degrees. The more you work on them *on the practice range,* the more they will fall into place during your play on the course. With sufficient practice they will become second-nature to you.

In short, regard your practice sessions as being times when you are feeding information and success patterns into the "computer"—your brain and nervous system. "Program" your computer on the practice green or tee, but once on the course, let your computer do the job of producing the swing "answer" you need for the shot at hand. If you consciously direct your computer as you swing, you'll merely foul up its circuitry. It will give you the wrong answer.

While your main concern on the course should be simply to play by feel, there are certain ways you can enhance your efforts and thus score even lower. During the rest of this chapter, I will pass along these stratagems, none of which will interfere with your basic method of merely visualizing shots and executing them by feel.

Your pace of living definitely affects your golf swing. I've seen professional men, after dashing around the office all day, rush out to the course for a "quick" lesson before dinner. They've been going helter-skelter for eight hours, and I'm supposed to slow down their golf swing in five minutes. No way! I can teach golf, but I can't change a person's metabolism.

I've known touring pros—Bobby Locke and, later, Gary Player, for example—who consciously try to do everything at half-speed before an important round of golf. They dress slowly, eat slowly, and drive to the course slowly. They'll leisurely hit a bucket of balls, stroke a few putts. By the time they tee it up on the first hole their entire pace of living that day will reflect itself favorably in the rhythm of their golf swing. It works for these players, and might help you as well.

Your wife might not like this piece of advice, but I don't think a golfer should do any heavy work around the house or in the garden within 24 hours of an important golf match. I'm a "green thumb" man myself. I love to plant flowers and trees on my day off. But if I do, the next day when I hold a golf club its grip feels thick. My hands feel stiff. They lack sensitivity.

I've also noticed that I tend to lose feel and rhythm if my hands and arms become cold. Even in slightly cool weather I make sure that I carry a hand-warmer. I also want my golf balls warm. This makes them easier to compress. More important, when I tee up a warm ball and feel its warmth, I sense subconsciously that I won't need to swing hard to compress it. I make a smoother swing.

You'll seldom see a touring pro eat a big meal immediately before a competitive round. He'll either eat a normal meal two or three hours beforehand, or just a light snack—a half-sandwich and some fruit, for instance—just before he tees it up. Too much food slows you down mentally and physically. Give it time to settle. And never eat a big lunch between nines—that is, if you care about how you play the rest of the round.

A good football team always goes onto the field with a "game plan," designed to capitalize on its strengths and the opponent's weaknesses. If the game plan is sound, and if the team executes properly, it will win—unless the opposing team has a better game plan and/or executes better.

Normally in golf you shouldn't consider the person or persons you are playing against as being your opponent. Your real "opponent" is the golf course itself. If you beat that opponent, you'll probably win your match. But to beat the course, you'll need a good game plan. And you'll need the self-discipline to stick with your plan. That's where most of us fail. We bogey or double-bogey two or three holes and we start taking chances. We go for the birdie, just like a football team that's losing often drops its game plan and goes for the long touchdown pass—the "bomb." When you go for the bomb in golf—when you try "hero" shots that have little chance to succeed, or when you press for a few extra yards of distance—that's when you end up shooting 95 instead of 85.

Size up your opponent—the course—before your round. Make your game plan realistic, based on your strengths and weaknesses and those of the course itself.

First, make it your goal to keep the ball in play off the tee on every hole, even if it feels like you're cutting back on the power of your swing. Keep 10 per cent of your power in your pocket. Also, keep track of how many fairways you actually hit during each round you play. Do the same for the number of greens you hit in regulation figures, and how many holes you par after missing the green. Keep track of how many holes you play in a row without three-putting.

All of this record-keeping is worthwhile. It helps you establish a realistic game plan based on your current abilities. It also helps you discover those areas of your game that need work. But most important, it forces you to play your best on the hole coming up, regardless of how badly you might have messed up the one you've just played. It forces you to stick to your game plan, and thus to play "within yourself."

I once had a pupil who was in the motion picture business. When I asked him what type of shot he'd like to hit, he replied, "A straight shot—perfectly straight."

"Have you ever made a 'perfect' movie?" I asked.

He admitted that he had not.

There is nothing wrong with trying to hit the ball perfectly straight, but the smart golfer is realistic enough to know that he won't hit it straight all the time, or even most of the time. You should realize your limitations and play within them. You may find that most of your shots tend to draw or fade slightly to the left or right. So long as they don't magnify into hooks or bad slices, I see no reason why you shouldn't expect your shots to curve a given amount in a known direction, and plan each to allow for the bend.

You can't be a perfectionist in golf and expect to succeed. You must learn to play only those shots you're fairly sure you can play successfully. If you come to a hole that doglegs to the left, but you aren't sure you can play a controlled right-to-left shot, then you'd better visualize it flying down the middle and try to hit it that way.

Learn to find a simple style of play that works. Don't let your ego lure you into trying a shot that you can't be fairly sure of making, no matter how spectacular it would be to pull it off. Remember that the course is your opponent and it's just sitting there inanimate. It can't humiliate you, but you can humiliate yourself.

In 1970 I played 16 holes of the best golf I've ever played in my life at the famed Old Course at St. Andrews, Scotland. I hit every green. I missed every bunker. Then I got carried away. I began thinking what my friends would think of me if I could finish par-birdie for a 66.

On 17, instead of playing short of the green and then chipping up for an easy par-putt, I tried to make a fantastic shot all the way to the narrow green. My ball flew over the green and onto the road—the worst possible place. I finished with a double-bogey six on the hole. Then I was so discouraged that I bogeyed 18. Instead of 66, I shot 70. On one shot my ego had caused me to discard my game plan. It had ruined a great round.

Yet, it was more than mere ego that ruined that round at St. Andrew's. The thought of shooting a 66 at this famous course that has frustrated so many great players had also created a form of tension inside of me.

Now, tension in golf is nothing to be ashamed of. Let's face it, the finest striker of the golf ball today has difficulty controlling his nerves on putts. I'm speaking of the great Ben Hogan. He controls a ball struck into the air better than any other human being, yet he has trouble controlling his nerves when he must roll the ball along the ground. If tension sometimes gets to Hogan, why should you feel ashamed if you occasionally "choke?" Everybody bows to tension in golf, sooner or later.

Your ability to control your nerves depends on many things, both physical and psychological. Generally speaking, I think a person who has struggled in life and has overcome hardship will handle tension better than someone who's had everything presented on a silver platter. Usually, the more you play under pressure, the better you become at coping with it. I knew I could make that $50,000 putt to win the 1954 World Championship of Golf because I'd faced similar situations on the pro tour. I don't mean I'd ever had a $50,000 putt, but I had been through situations earlier in my career where failure to succeed on a given shot represented an even greater threat to myself and my family. If I had that same putt today, after years away from active competition, I doubt that I could control my nerves nearly so well.

Sometimes the cause of tension is less obvious. Maybe the shape or terrain of a certain hole bothers you. Certain shot situations may recall to your mind past failures under similar circumstances. A bad lie might psych you out. So might the wind in your face, or some dirt on your ball, or an airplane flying overhead.

Anything that causes tension tends to make you do two things. First, it tends to make you grip the club tighter than normal, either at address or at some point in your swing. Second, it causes you to alter the basic rhythm of your swing. It usually makes you swing faster than normal.

To ease tension, or to minimize its effect, I suggest you try these tips.

First, after you've visualized your shot and imagined how your swing should feel, take a deep breath and then exhale slowly and fully, relaxing your hand, arm and shoulder muscles as you do.

Next hold the club with a grip that seems slightly lighter than normal.

Finally, merely swing as smoothly and as rhythmically as you can to produce the shot you've visualized.

You'll also find it helpful to heed the advice of the great Bobby Jones. He found that during the first few holes of a tournament round it helped if he tried not to knock the ball too far. Instead, he merely tried to feel the pace, the rhythm, of his swing. Then he'd gradually start letting out for more distance as his mind and muscles became acclimated to the course, the conditions of pressure, the people, the pattern of his shots and so on.

There will be times on the course when you seem to lose your basic swing rhythm. When this happens, you should modify your club selection in a way that forces you to make an easier, less-forced swing at the ball. If you are on the tee for a drive, for instance, consider using a 3-wood instead, if that club makes you produce a smoother, easier swing. Or, if you have, say, a 7-iron shot to the green, use your 6-iron. This will force you to swing with a smoother, seemingly slower, rhythm. If you do this for a few shots, you'll soon regain your normal swing pace.

Another thing that will help you find lost rhythm is to swing through the ball at the same pace that you used on your practice swing. You should always use your practice swing as a preview for your regular swing, rather than merely as a warm-up swing to loosen your muscles. Try to make your practice swing just as rhythmical and smooth and well-timed as you can. Then merely duplicate it on your swing *through*—not *at*—the ball.

Many golfers make better swings with a 3-wood or 4-wood off the fairway than they do with a driver on a tee shot. I think one reason is that the club-heads of the fairway woods are shallower and a bit more lofted than is the driver. They give the impression that they will slide "under" the ball and readily sweep it into the air. Thus the golfer makes an easier, smoother swing without feeling that he must scoop under the ball to lift it off the ground. I see no reason why any golfer who feels more comfortable with a 3-wood shouldn't use it on his drives.

Other golfers would make a better swing with a 5-wood and a 6-wood than with a 2-iron and a 3-iron on fairway shots. They look down at the thin blade and small face on these long irons and automatically sense that they must swing harder to make the ball fly far. They unconsciously increase their grip pressure, create tension, and actually curtail clubhead speed.

Judging distance on the course is largely a matter of experience—you learn to look at the terrain and more or less sense what club you'll need. But you should be aware of a few gimmicks that can help when you are in doubt:

Don't be deceived by a dip in the fairway. These depressions invariably make shots look shorter than they really are. You'll need more club than seems apparent.

Learn to look at trees and bushes around the green. Often they'll give you a better feel for distance than will the flagstick itself.

Learn to watch the flight of the approach shots of your playing partners. As these shots fly to the green, assess in your own mind if they are going to fall short or long, or land near the pin. If you judge the trajectories of these shots incorrectly, you then modify your club selection accordingly.

Most golfers seem to expect to hit their shots farther than they really can with any degree of accuracy. If you stand by a green at your club and watch several groups of players hit their approach shots, you'll find that at least 80 per cent of the shots will finish short of the flagstick. Only about 15 per cent will finish on the green past the hole. Only about 5 per cent will run or carry over the green.

Failure to hit approach shots all the way to the hole is due partly to a fear of going over the green and partly to an unrealistic attitude about how far you can expect to hit shots with a given club.

Very few club golfers have really trained themselves to hit the ball all the way to the flagstick on approach shots from, say, 50 yards on out. They'll play "run-up golf," even though the vast majority of your sand bunkers are placed around the front and front-side portions of the green. These same golfers will "ooh" and "ah" at tournaments when they see the pros throw their approaches all the way to the flagstick, but they won't try it themselves.

Hitting to the flagstick is simply a matter of visualizing your shot carrying that far, and then conditioning yourself to using more club than you think you need. Once you get into the habit of using plenty of club to carry the ball all the way to the hole, you'll automatically be making a smoother swing with a constant, light grip pressure. You'll hit more shots squarely. They'll fly straighter and "bite" better.

One exception to the rule of carrying shots to the flagstick is, as I've mentioned, the chip shot. Whenever possible within, say, 50 feet of the green, use a less-lofted club and play a low shot that lands just onto the green and runs up to the hole. As mentioned, this type of shot allows you to make a shorter, simpler stroke with a less-lofted club, than you could on the fuller swing required by a highly-lofted club. And, as noted, most golfers find it simpler to hit shots a prescribed distance if they roll the ball along the ground—as in putting—than if they fly it through the air.

Another time when you might forsake the practice of carrying your approach shot all the way to the flagstick is when the green is sharply contoured. Then you must select the spot on the green from which you will have your easiest putt. Visualize your approach flying all the way to that spot, and play it accordingly.

If the hole is cut near the edge of the green near a hazard or a steep slope, you might select a spot nearer the center of the green as your target, even though the hole itself may be 20 feet farther forward, or even farther away off to the side. Where to aim depends on how much confidence you have in your ability to judge distance correctly and hit the shot accurately. I've found that most amateur golfers tend towards over-confidence. They don't give themselves enough margin for error.

One of the best ways to cut strokes from your score—along with practicing your putting—is mastering a wide variety of shots with your fairway and sand wedges. Learn to play low shots, high shots, soft shots, crisp shots, shots from rough, shots from close lies, uphill shots, downhill, side-hill, etc.

You can master your wedges at home by trying to land your shots in a bucket or basket. Shoot from all different angles and distances and lies. Ten or 20 minutes of this practice every day will do wonders for increasing the sensitivity in your hands and your feel for distance and timing. In two weeks you'll find your scores becoming noticeably lower. Just make sure as you practice that you imagine beforehand how each shot will look and feel.

One of the advantages of playing by feel is that you can't help but rapidly improve your short game—your chipping and putting.

First, learning to play by feel, as we have seen, starts with putts and short shots. This method of learning also requires going back to these shots whenever you lose your basic rhythm and timing. Thus, playing by feel calls for more putting and chipping practice than you've probably been doing.

Second, playing by feel requires that you visualize beforehand how your putt or chip shots will break with the terrain. Playing by feel forces you to make a positive decision about your intended line.

Once you've made this decision, you're free to forget about your line and stress hitting the shot the correct distance. You'll do this in the normal course of playing by feel, as you sense how the shot you've visualized should feel when being properly executed. This freedom to concentrate on distance is bound to reduce the number of times you take three shots to get down from on or just off the green.

I think you'll also find it helpful to own two putters, one heavier than the other. Use the light putter on fast greens, the heavy putter on slow surfaces. Thus you'll be able to maintain more or less the same pace of stroke and the same grip pressure on all greens, regardless of their texture.

My main goal in this book has been to describe a simple way for you to vastly improve your golfing skills. Learning to play by feel will require work at first, but in the end you will swing better and score better with much less effort. You will derive greater satisfaction from your game than you've ever dreamed possible.

And that brings me to my final word of advice. Accept golf as a challenge, as a means of proving yourself *to* yourself. But never lose sight of the fact that your time on the course should be enjoyable. Never forget that golf is, most certainly, above all, a *game.*